50
COLORADO
SKI TOURS

by
Richard DuMais

Published by
High Peak Publishing
Boulder, Colorado

Section maps courtesy of U.S.G.S.
Photos by the author
Typesetting and Composition by Graphic Directions, Boulder, Colorado
Printed by Empire Printing, Boulder, Colorado

Published by High Peak Publishing
Box 4804
Boulder, Colorado 80306

As soon as man binds long pieces of wood to his feet he conquers the birds in their flight, the swiftest running dogs, and the reindeer that run twice as fast as the deer.

—The King's Mirror

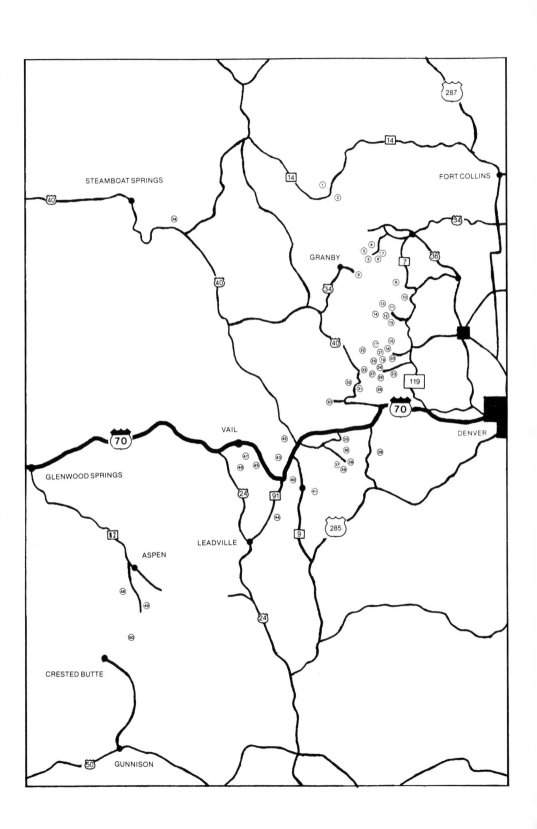

INTRODUCTION

Probably more than any other single area the mountains of Colorado are known as Ski-Country. Their beautiful mountains, good weather, and good snow are world reknowned. In recent years as well as being a mecca for downhill skiers, Colorado has become increasingly, a major center for ski touring. With the increased popularity of cross-country skiing the number of local skiers has risen dramatically, as has the number of visitors participating in this pastime. For many years people have toured throughout the state and many of the tours have become established over this period as popular and traditional outings. Others have risen to new levels of popularity with the development of various aspects of the sport. Over the years many of these have been recorded in various local guides or pamphlets as well as through articles in different magazines and journals, and more recently in a number of books covering different parts of the state. This book consists of fifty tours throughout the state. These are primarily located within a reasonable driving distance of the major metropolitan area of the state and are accessible to the bulk of the cross-country skiers of the region. Consequently, while the tours are spread out around the state, approximately ½ of them are in the Front Range.

Due to the limitations of time and space the tours have been selected on the basis of their popularity and appeal. This text does not purport to present a complete selection of tours by any means. In fact, in many of the areas the one or two trips described can only serve as an introduction to that region. These tours are all quite well known and most of them have been widely used for many years. It is hoped that these routes will enable skiers unfamiliar with the various areas to enjoy them and get to know them better. Also the tours range a great deal in difficulty and length so that skiers of all levels can find trips that are compatible with their abilities.

SEASONS, WEATHER, AND CONDITIONS

The ski touring season in Colorado generally extends from December until April. This of course is dependent on the weather and the season of the tours in this book varies from year to year and is also related to the location of the specific tours. Those situated on or near high passes usually come into condition earlier and have good snow and skiing much later. Those lower down, especially if they have a sunny exposure, or areas that tend to be blown clear by the wind much of the time and hence have less snow, will have a shorter season. Occasionally there is good skiing as early as mid-November and some years the snow lingers in skiable quantities in the mountains as late as May or even June, but this is not normally the case.

In the Colorado Rockies wind is often a very important weather factor. This is especially true along the Front Range. High winds also seem more prevalent early in the winter and they are more of a factor in the eastern ranges than further west. This of course is a general assesment and not a hard and fast rule. High winds not only can be unpleasant but they also are important in determining the snow conditions.

In general, the short days of the early season (through December into January) have colder and more harsh weather and the snow base is not as deep or consolidated. During this period the snow tends to be very cold and light and dry. From mid-January through February, as the weather improves, the skiing is more pleasant and unless there is a shortage of snow this is often the best part of the season. By March temperatures are rising and conditions can start to vary a lot. March and early April often see big snowfalls as well as warmer, sunnier days and while things tend to fluctuate more, this time period often will feature exceptional days of skiing. Normally from mid-April on spring conditions will prevail. As stated earlier these of course vary a great deal from year to year.

To more specifically determine conditions one can check with local outdoor shops dealing with ski gear. Also the weather reports or a downhill ski report gives one a good indication of what current snow or weather conditions are like. The park headquarters at Rocky Mountain National Park can inform one what snow conditions are like for that area. One other good source of information is the highway road report for driving conditions. This is especially informative concerning the passes around the state.

EQUIPMENT AND SAFETY

While it is not the intention of this book to serve as an instruction manual on cross-country skiing technique or equipment a few general words are appropriate. The tours described here have been done by people using virtually every type of ski gear imaginable. This varies greatly and is dependent on ones personal style and preferences. The longest and most severe tours described have been done by skiers using ultra-light nordic racing gear and conversely, one occasionally sees people on the easiest and shortest trails with heavy alpine touring type gear. Most skiers will find that general purpose light touring or touring gear will more than adequately suffice for these trips. Medium range skis and boots with pin bindings are what most people will prefer. This of course is subjective and in the end whatever one feels most comfortable with is probably the best choice. It is a good idea to carry a back up of a few spare parts in case of emergency repairs.

The same ideas are true with clothing. Most of these outings are at a fairly high elevation and severe conditions can be encountered. The seriousness of the conditions outdoors increase greatly in winter and the weather can change a lot even in the course of a few hours. Even on nice days one should carry adequate clothing and equipment for the trip being undertaken. Good advice on this matter can be sought at the numerous mountaineering and ski shops around the state. Likewise, there are many books on the subject that will comprehensively cover this subject.

Water is often overlooked by people traveling out in the mountains in winter. The exercise and elevation can dehydrate one a great deal and it is best to always carry food and water along. Streams and lakes are frozen or snow covered so locating water en route is not often easy. In addition such things as sunglasses, sunscreen, and a few first aid items are a good idea as are a map of the region and a compass. As well as carrying these latter items one should be familiar with their use.

Those unfamiliar with cross-country ski techniques or winter travel are encouraged to gain instruction in these activities. There are many books out on this field of recreation and also there are many touring centers and instructional services around the state which offer a wide choice and variety of services.

The last subject to be covered in this section is avalanches. On most of the tours described these are simply not a factor. Whenever possible hazard might exist it has been mentioned in the description. This does not mean that under exceptional conditions a further potential might not exist. In most all cases areas of potential hazard can be best dealt with simply by staying well away from them or not going in dangerous areas when a hazard exists. While this may sound overly simplistic it is probably the surest and least complex approach. Those unsure of the situation or after recent snowfalls can easily check on conditions by inquiring through the local Forest Service Office. Those seeking further information are advised to read any of several books on the matter or to take classes offered by numerous groups.

REGULATIONS AND ETHICS

While many of these tours are on public land and no specific rules and regulations apply this is not the case with all of them. The tours in Rocky Mountain National Park are all subject to the regulations of the park. Most notably no dogs are allowed and overnight use is strictly regulated. Those skiers using the park should be familiar with the rules of that region. Many of the outings cross private property or are adjacent to it. One should respect this and abide by any posted notices, etc. Also several of the trips originating at the East Portal area require access across private land which is currently restricted. This should be observed and one is refered to the discussion accompanying tour #24 concerning this matter.

A few of the tours described lead to or involve the use of huts. The use of the Alfred Braun Hut System near Aspen is very limited and requires special permission. See tour #50 for further details. When using any hut please keep it clean and do not damage the buildings or their contents. Kindly abide by any rules concerning their use or permits, fees, etc.

All of these areas are heavily used and one should be considerate of others when using them. Park in such a way as not to block access or traffic and abide by any parking regulation signs. When using trails please refrain from leaving garbage and trash along the trail. The same applies to human excretions. If you stop along a well used trail, try to do so in such a manner that you do not block the way for others. One last point of discussion is dogs. While you may love your animal, the rest of the world does not necessarily share your affection. Dogs destroy a ski track completely as they walk along it, they do not discriminate between the trail and elsewhere when they defecate and are very annoying to other skiers. Leave your dog at home!

HOW TO USE THIS BOOK

When using this book one will notice that the route descriptions consist of three major divisions. The first is a small list of pertinent data directly below the title. This gives the basic essential details of the tour. The second part is a written discussion and more detailed description of the tour. The third part is a reproduction of a portion of a USGS topographic map.

The first part of the description has six subjects listed. The first of these is the grade. This is a relative grade and there are three catagories: easy, moderate, and difficult. Various factors figure into the grade of a route, the location and elevation, length, steepness and technical level of skiing skill involved, and the overall seriousness of the tour. Easy graded tours are those suitable for beginners and inexperienced skiers or those people looking for an easy trip. The moderate grade implies a somewhat more difficult trip. Most skiers with experience will find this level quite managable. The difficult tours all have some more serious aspect. Usually they are longer, harder to do or follow, steeper, and require a higher level of experience and expertise. They are intended for skiers with more experience and who can handle the less difficult tours without problems. Needless to say there is also a fair amount of latitude within each classification.

The distance is just what the term implies. As most of the tours ski out to a point and then back the distance is given for one way only. When planning these tours one should remember this and realize that the return trip will double this figure. Several of the trips do not retrace themselves and are loop tours, or start and finish at separate points. In these cases the distance given is for the entire trip. In such cases the distance is indicated as being for a one way trip.

The elevation change will indicate the net amount of change in elevation. It shows the difference between the highest and lowest points of a tour and can be a general reference as to the type of relief one will encounter.

The high point figure denotes the elevation of the highest point on the tour. From this figure one can realize the elevation range involved. The altitude is important as it relates closely to the seriousness of the outing and the general situation of the tour.

The term approximate time expresses a general figure for the amount of time for the entire trip. This is intended to refer to average parties of appropriate ability for the tour involved and is for conditions one can normally expect to encounter.

The last catagory is the USGS topographic maps. This lists the topo maps that cover the area involved in that tour. These refer to 7.5 minute series maps.

The verbal description usually starts with a general discussion of the tour. This will hopefully give the reader a feel for the trip and an overall picture of what to expect. Any special factors such as seasonal aspects, problems with access, potential hazards, transportation considerations, and other unique features are noted. In the descriptions themselves the route is described as the skier will see it while doing the trip. Left and right are relative to the direction one should be heading at that time, and often these are further clarified by the addition of compass directions. Milages are often interjected, and it should be mentioned that these are approximate.

The maps included have been reproduced from relevant sections of USGS topographic quadrangle maps. Most of them are from 7.5 min. series maps, though the map for tour #28 is from a 15 min. series map. Also the maps accompanying tour #5 and tour #8 are from the

USGS map of Rocky Mountain National Park. The maps make good references but it is preferable to have the actual quadrangles and parties are advised to carry them.

On the maps the routes have been drawn in and additional figures and symbols added. These are lised below with the appropriate explanations.

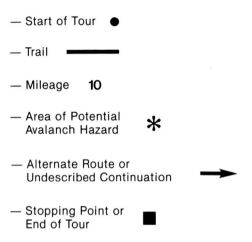

— Start of Tour   ●

— Trail   ▬▬▬

— Mileage   **10**

— Area of Potential
  Avalanch Hazard   ✳

— Alternate Route or
  Undescribed Continuation   ➡

— Stopping Point or
  End of Tour   ■

In conclusion it should be stated that this book is merely intended as a general reference to the routes and is not a substitute for ones own judgement or route finding abilities. Winter conditions are very changeable and while references have been selected that should be stable these may alter or become obscured due to the weather or unusual amounts of snow. Hopefully this book will serve as an aid to ones enjoyment of the outdoors and mountains of Colorado, which was the intent with which it was written. A book such as this can not be written without help from many different directions and thanks are extended to all who aided in any way with its conception, development, and completion. But most of all thanks to all those who have participated in these tours.

Contents

1 MONTGOMERY PASS

Grade: Moderate
Distance: 2 Miles—One Way
Elevation Change: 1,050 Feet
High Point: 11,000 Feet
Approximate Time: One-half Day
USGS Topographic Map:
  Clark Peak

Now that the Cameron Pass road is being kept open in winter, it provides access to a large and significant area for skiing and winter recreation. The area near Cameron Pass has abundant snowfall and the high ridges and valleys of this region collect and hold snow relatively early in the season. Good skiing can usually be found here as early as mid November and it continues well into April. As the terrain is often steep and open skiers should pay attention to the risk posed by avalanches.

The Montgomery Pass Trail is just north of Cameron Pass and this short steep ski tour is quite popular. Those choosing to do this trip will be rewarded for the steep ascent with good views and a fast and exciting downhill run back to the road.

From Rt. 287 north of Fort Collins drive west on Rt. 14 for 60 miles to Chambers Lake. Six miles beyond Chambers Lake and 2¼ miles northeast of Cameron Pass one pulls off at the Zimmerman Lake parking area. This is on the east side of the road and just southwest of a reservoir/lake.

At the lower (northeast) end of the parking area there are trail signs. Go west across the road to the start of the Montgomery Pass trail. The tour starts up this trail which angles up into the woods and is marked by triangular blue blazes. Climb steeply through the trees as the trail roughly takes a line following the south edge of the Montgomery Creek drainage. After about one mile the angle of the ascent lessens though it still continues steadily upwards.

Cross a small dip and pass an old cabin. Soon the trail reaches the edge of the trees and one should head up and slightly to the right (northwest) across open slopes to reach Montgomery Pass. The pass is a low saddle on the crest of the ridge and is often wind swept and bare.

The descent to the road is fast and steep and one has a choice of which specific route to take. The most apparent is simply to ski back down the trail. Many parties prefer to descend slightly to the northeast and then to head straight on down the Montgomery Creek drainage. At about the 10,200' level this drainage narrows and is blocked by trees. At this point one can ski off to the right (south) leaving the drainage proper. This is usually marked by red flags and soon leads one to the trail which is close by and which is then followed on down to the road. A third possible route of descent is to head down in a southeasterly direction from the pass to descend a drainage south of the trail and parallel to it.

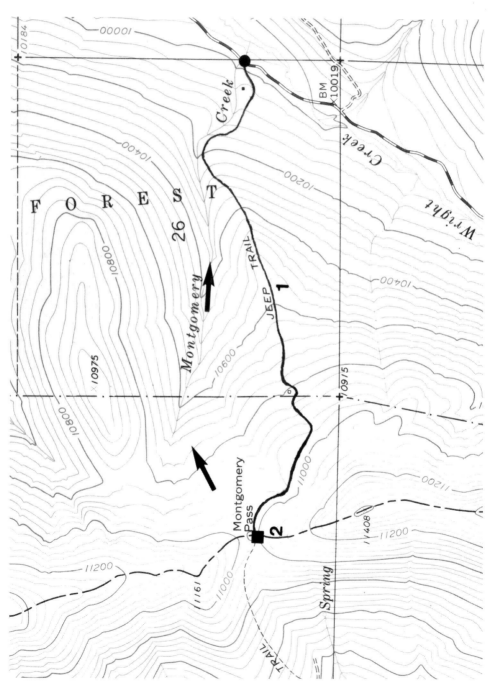

2 UPPER MICHIGAN DITCH

Grade: Easy
Distance: 1½ Miles—One Way
Elevation Change: 120 Feet
High Point: 10,300 Feet
Approximate Time: One-quarter Day
USGS Topographic Map:
   Clark Peak
   Chambers Lake

Like the preceding tour the Upper Michigan Ditch often has good snow early in the season. One often finds good skiing here by mid November. Its sheltered aspect and sunny exposure on good days combine with the nearly flat skiing to make it an excellent trip for beginning skiers. The route is along an obvious dirt road and route finding poses no problems.

The tour is all below tree line, though not heavily wooded. The tour, as it is described here, is quite short, only about 3 miles round trip. This distance is quite arbitrary and those seeking a longer tour of this standard can extend the trip by simply skiing along the ditch for a greater distance. One can even continue to one of the high lakes further on and those seeking steeper and more challenging skiing sometimes ascend the hillside on the east side of the road. This is best done at about the ¾ mile point where a drainage comes down from the east. These big southwest facing slopes provide steep and exciting downhill runs and lead the skier right back to the road along Michigan Ditch.

To reach the start of the tour drive along Rt. 14 all the way to Cameron Pass. Park in a large well marked parking area on the northwest side of the highway. Head southeast across Rt. 14 to the start of a good, wide trail that is really an old jeep road. This heads up along the valley following the Michigan Ditch as it traverses the long southwest facing hillside.

Ski up this trail which seems nearly flat but which very gradually gains elevation over the course of the tour. Below and to the right one can see the highway along the valley bottom. After ¾ of a mile a steep drainage is crossed which comes down from the left. For the next ½ mile the tour continues along the road with very little change. At that point the trail curves to the left following the contour of the hillside and proceeds up the valley of the Michigan River. Continue along the road as it turns more easterly. The skiing continues nearly level and much the same for another ¼ mile. At this point one reaches some old broken-down buildings. This is an obvious stopping point and the tour is described as ending here.

Those wishing to extend the ski can continue on to the southeast along the jeep road. The return trip to the highway simply reverses the trip described. The run out along one's tracks is all slightly downhill and goes quickly and easily.

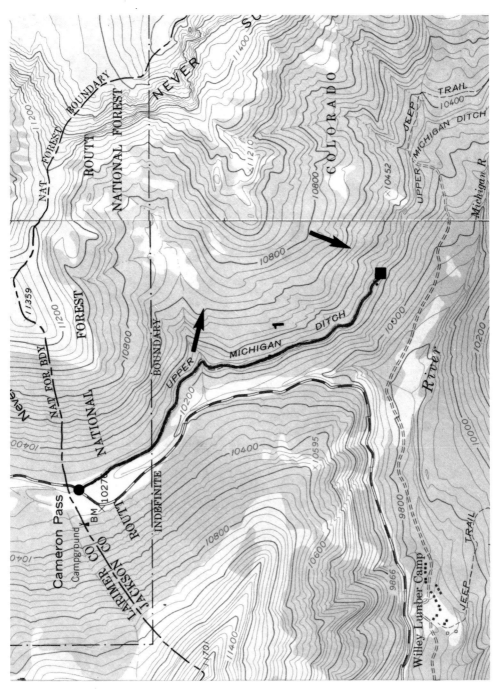

3 BEAR LAKE-EMERALD LAKE

Grade: Easy-Moderate
Distance: 2 Miles—One Way
Elevation Change: 825 Feet
High Point: 10,125 Feet
Approximate Time: One-half Day
USGS Topographic Map:
McHenrys Peak

This tour is located amidst some of the most spectacular scenery in Rocky Mountain National Park. Though not a very long trip it combines a steady uphill climb going in with a fast downhill run on the return trip. The Bear Lake area is usually crowded, especially on weekends, but even a short distance from the parking area the number of people is greatly diminished. The high starting elevation in conjunction with the often inclement weather and winds require one to be prepared for potentially severe conditions.

Start the tour from the Bear Lake parking area. This is reached by turning off the main park road ¼ mile west of the Beaver Meadows entrance station. Follow the Bear Lake road for 9 miles to its end at a large parking area just below and east of the lake itself.

From the upper right corner of the parking lot head up toward the lake. One can follow an easy trail that circles Bear Lake to have a short and easy tour. Most skiers will want to continue to Emerald Lake however, a longer and more rewarding outing. To do this, turn left (south) just before the lake and ski along a trail past the summer ranger cabin. Soon the trail forks. The left fork leads down to the Glacier Gorge trailhead. Take the right fork and climb steadily up along a hillside which slopes down to the left. The trail levels out soon and curves around to the right. This shortly leads to Nymph Lake, at the ½ mile point of the tour.

Either follow the trail around the right side of Nymph Lake or cross it directly. A short distance beyond the lake the trail switchbacks up left, passing below some rock outcrops that are above and northwest of the lake. Continue contouring up and west, rising above the drainage. One can also cut left at the lake's south end, heading up directly to this same approximate location. Keep climbing up along the open hillside as the drainage narrows and steepens. A short steep section up this and over a low ridge leads to Dream Lake at about the 1 mile mark.

Cross the lake, if solidly frozen, or else along its right shore to the far end and continue up the valley following the main stream bed and its right bank. Climb a short steep section to the right of a rocky outcrop and then ski through alternating clearings and trees over rolling terrain staying to the right of the stream. Reach the top of a low rise and then descend to Emerald Lake which is just beyond.

Return to the parking area by skiing back down following ones tracks or the main drainage. Take care near Nymph Lake not to descend too far but to cut back left to pick up the trail.

10

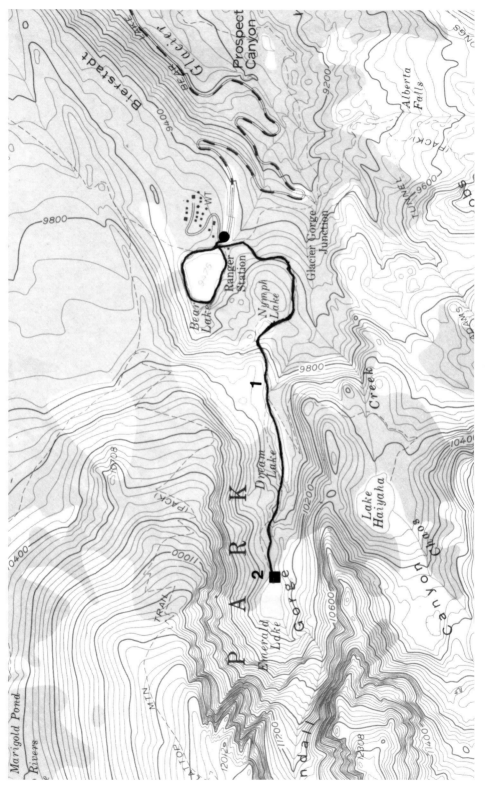

4 BEAR LAKE TO HALLOWELL PARK

Grade: Moderate
Distance: 4¼ Miles—One Way Trip
Elevation Change: 1,136 Foot Loss
High Point: 9,760 Feet
Approximate Time: One-half Day or Less
USGS Topographic Map:
  McHenrys Peak
  Longs Peak

This is a fast and exciting tour often done several times in one day or as a short outing. It is sheltered and in the trees most of the way and after the short initial section of uphill the rest of the trip is all downhill. A car shuttle back to the start should be arranged unless one plans to hitch a ride back to Bear Lake. Most parties do one or the other as the prospect of the long steady climb back up along the trail, complicated by the threat of more skiers hurtling down at you is not very appealing.

Just west of the Beaver Meadows entrance station turn south onto the Bear Lake road. Drive for 3½ miles along this to a large U-curve. This is Hallowell Park and the end of the tour. Continue 5½ more miles to the end of the road at a large parking lot at Bear Lake.

Start by skiing around the right (east) side of Bear Lake. After a short distance the Flattop Mountain trail turns off to the right. This is well marked and climbs up over a small rise and then curves back to the left passing through some boulders. Beyond these the trail slants up to the right along an aspen covered hillside to a trail junction. The trail up Flattop cuts sharply back up to the left. This trip takes the right fork which goes straight ahead and continues to the top of the morainal ridge at about ½ mile from the start of the tour. The trail flattens out as it curves left through the woods and then back to the right as it crosses the low ridge top and starts down.

The trail descends steeply and continuously through pine forest for the next ½ mile. At that point a turnoff to Bierstadt Lake is passed heading off to the right. Another ½ mile of similar terrain and skiing brings one to the second Bierstadt Lake turnoff, also on the right. Continue straight on down the trail as it winds steadily and steeply down through the woods to reach Mill Creek Basin. From this point the trail parallels Mill Creek as the skiing levels off. After a short while one enters a series of open meadows and heads east and northeast through these to reach Hallowell Park and the Bear Lake road.

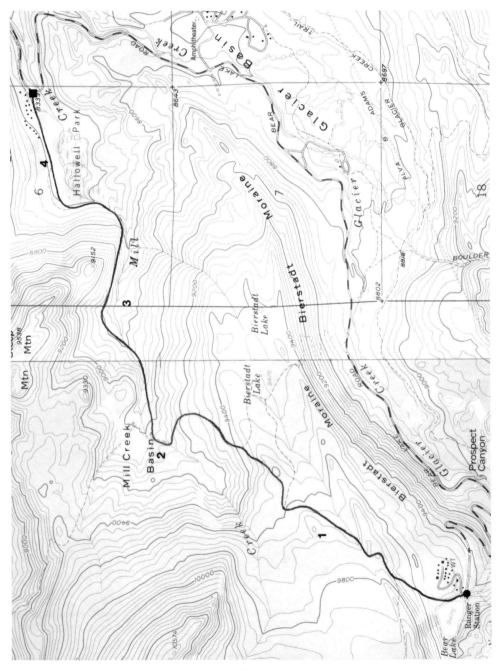

5 ODESSA GORGE

Grade: Difficult
Distance: 9½ Miles—One Way Trip
Elevation Change: 1,400 Foot Loss
High Point: 10,650 Feet
Approximate Time: 1 Day
USGS Topographic Map:
  McHenrys Peak
  Longs Peak

This tour is one of the better and longer tours in Rocky Mountain National Park. Being long and challenging, parties should be sure to allocate sufficient time for the trip. It offers spectacular scenery and quite difficult skiing. The conditions can be extremely variable as the tour progresses and unfortunately the snow cover is usually sparse on the lower sections of the trip. The tour starts at Bear Lake and ends in Moraine Park so return transportation must be planned.

Just west of the Beaver meadows entrance station turn south onto the Bear Lake road. Drive 1¼ miles further and turn right onto the Moraine Park road. Go about ½ mile on this and turn left and follow this road to a carpark at the end of the plowed road. Leave a car here and return to the Bear Lake road and drive on up this to its end at the large parking area at Bear Lake.

Start by skiing for a short distance around the right (east) side of Bear Lake and turn right onto the well marked Flattop Mountain trail. The trail goes over a small rise, curves back left and passes through some boulders, and then slants up an aspen covered hillside to a trail junction ½ mile from the start. Turn sharply left and follow the Flattop Mountain trail up the south facing hillside above Bear Lake. Soon one reaches the top of a ridge and crosses to its right side, contouring above an open, boulder filled valley. Shortly the trail reenters the woods and another trail junction is reached. Take the right fork which goes on to Lake Helene and Fern and Odessa lakes. Climb gradually, heading northwest, as the trail passes steep slopes down to the right and some open viewpoints.

Stay on this course, mostly in the trees, and gaining elevation as the trail leads on around the base of Flattop. Eventually one leaves the trees and crosses a series of open meadows below the north slopes of this mountain, staying near the treeline. At a little past the 2 mile mark the valley narrows and one passes Marigold Lake and then Two Rivers Lake. Either go around the right side of the latter or cross it directly and continue on to soon reach Lake Helene.

For a short ways beyond this point the route finding can be a little tricky. From the north end of Lake Helene the trail goes off to the right. Do not follow this summer route. Instead a short steep gully just on the left beyond the lake enables one to descend through the rocky headwall and reach the upper end of the valley below. Once down this section ski on down the open and rolling slopes to the creek drainage leading on to Odessa Lake 3½ miles from the start of the tour. Cross to the lower end of Odessa Lake and enter the narrow exit drainage of Fern Creek. This quickly steepens and gives one a fast and exciting downhill run before it levels off and curves to the right. Either continue along the stream bed or down along its right bank to reach Fern Lake. Ski to the left around this lake past some cabins. Just beyond these, at the east end of the lake, pick up the trail again. This descends steeply and continuously in a series of switchbacks for 1½ miles to Spruce Canyon and The Pool.

Cross the bridge over the stream below The Pool and follow the trail along the left side of the stream. The last 3 miles descends gradually along the bottom of this valley and is often bare of snow and may necessitate walking. Eventually the trail ends and a last stretch on a dirt road brings one to the carpark at the end of the plowed road in Moraine Park.

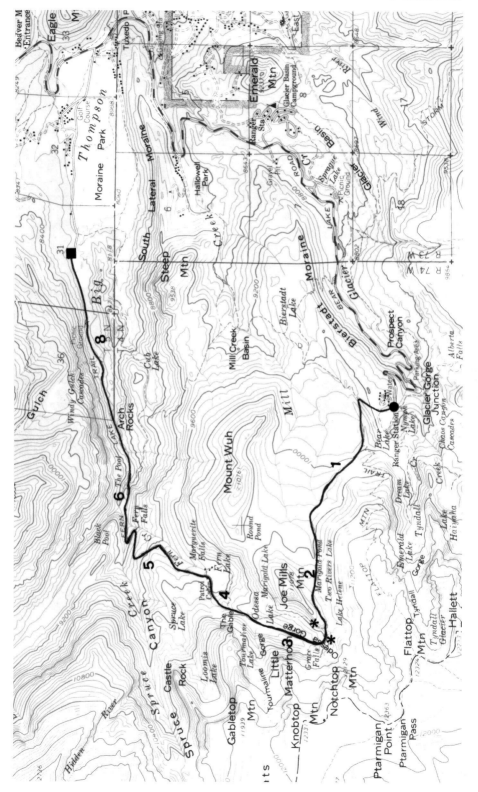

6 THE LOCH

Grade: Moderate-Difficulat
Distance: 1.9 Miles—One Way
Elevation Change: 900 Feet
High Point: 10,160 Feet
Approximate Time: One-half Day
USGS Topographic Map:
  McHenrys Peak

The short, steep climb up to the Loch provides quick access to the spectacular high mountain scenery of this part of Rocky Mountain National Park. The cirques beyond the Loch are attractive to skiers seeking longer and more adventurous ski touring and the descent back to the Glacier Gorge trailhead is fast and exciting.

Drive ¼ mile west of the Beaver Meadows park entrance and turn south onto the Bear Lake road. Proceed along this for 8¼ miles to the Glacier Gorge trailhead parking area.

Start by crossing the road and skiing a short way up to some signs. Go left along the Glacier Gorge trail which contours southeast, crossing a small brook, to reach a wooden bridge with railings. At this point the tour turns to the right, leaving the trail, and heads up the wide and prominent drainage. This is fairly open with scattered trees and bushes. Gradual climbing at first is followed by a short steep section beyond which one crosses a shallow beaver pond and continues up the open stream bed to reenter the woods. The valley then curves slightly left, passing between the Glacier Knobs. At slightly over 1 mile one intersects the main trail.

Go right on this trail past an outhouse and the turnoff for the summer trail to Lake Haiyaha. Ski on past a summer stockpen and on to a bridge crossing the stream coming down Loch Vale. Go straight up Loch Vale beyond the bridge, following the streambed in its narrow drainage. For ½ mile the climb is gradual with short steeper steps. Beyond this the drainage widens slightly and one reaches a steep slope with cliffs on either side.

Zigzag up this slope and continue over the drifted ridge just beyond it to reach the Loch. The very last short little run down to the lake itself is often very windy and drifted hardpack. One can continue to the far end of the Loch and up the streambed of its inlet to ski on to either Sky Pond or the Andrews Glacier valley. Most parties simply stop at the Loch. The descent follows the same route and is a fast and rather continuous downhill run all the way back to the car.

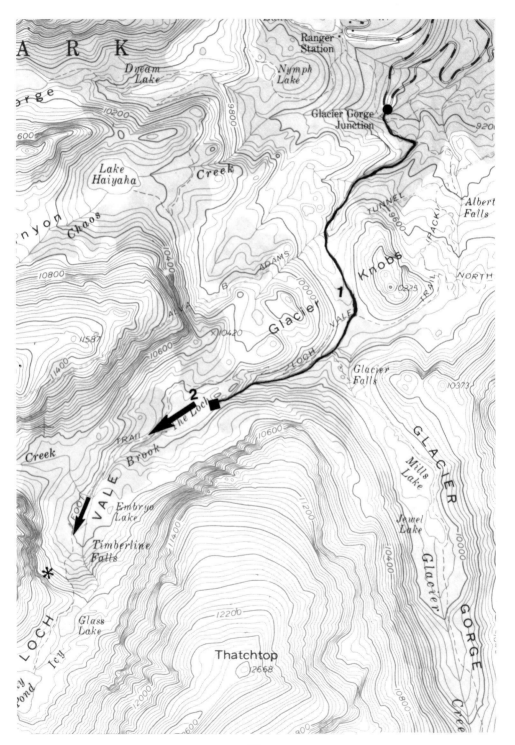

7 BLACK LAKE

Grade: Difficult
Distance: 4 Miles—One Way
Elevation Change: 1,400 Feet
High Point: 10,600 Feet
Approximate Time: One Day
USGS Topographic Map:
  McHenrys Peak

Glacier Gorge is one of the real beauty spots of Rocky Mountain National Park. This fairly long tour offers both good skiing and outstanding scenery in a high mountain setting. Sections of the tour can be very windy and often bare and exposed, especially at Mills Lake, but with good snow it is an exceptional ski trip. Care should be taken if crossing Mills Lake to be sure that the lake is frozen sufficiently to make crossing the ice safe.

Drive ¼ mile west of the Beaver Meadows entrance station and turn south onto the Bear Lake road. Drive up this for 8¼ miles to the Glacier Gorge trailhead parking area. Cross the road and ski up a short way to signs. Go left along the obvious Glacier Gorge trail as it contours around to the southeast, crossing a small brook, to reach a bridge. Leave the summer trail at this point turning right up an open drainage with bushes and trees. Ski up this past some short sections of climbing and cross a shallow beaver pond and then on to reenter the woods beyond. Follow the drainage as it turns

left and passes between the Glacier Knobs. At slightly more than 1 mile one intersects the summer trail.

Go right along this trail past an outhouse and the summer turnoff to Lake Haiyaha. Continue on past a summer stockpen to a bridge across the stream coming down from Loch Vale. Go left and cross the bridge and then up a short climb as the trail contours along the hillside and then climbs up onto a slabby ridge. Proceed along this to another bridge across the stream.

Either follow the trail as it climbs up a gully to the left and then go up to the right, over a low ridge to reach Mills Lake or veer to the right at the bridge and go up the stream drainage itself to reach the lake. Cross the lake directly if the ice is safe or ski along its lefthand shoreline to the far end. Continue on a short distance further to reach Jewel Lake at the 2 mile mark.

The next 1½ miles of skiing follows the stream drainage up Glacier Gorge. At first one goes along the left side of the stream but soon one skis up the streambed itself. After this one reaches a series of steep open slopes that lead up in several steps to Black Lake. One can stop at the lake or ski around its left side to a long snowfilled gully. This can be ascended to reach the wide and spectacular upper part of Glacier Gorge.

The descent back to the parking area follows one's tracks on down the valley. This return trip usually goes quite quickly and when packed or icy it can be very fast and tricky.

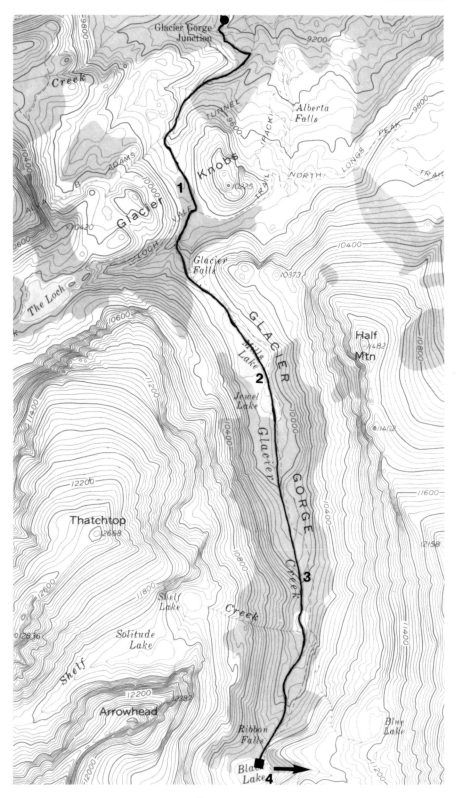

8 WILD BASIN

Grade: Easy-Difficult
Distance: 8½ Miles—One Way
Elevation Change: 2,225 Feet
High Point: 10,574 Feet
Approximate Time: One Day
USGS Topographic Map:
  Allens Park
  Isolation Peak

The overall difficulty of this trip will vary a great deal depending on snow conditions and also on how far one chooses to ski. With good snow coverage a short tour into the end of the road or one of the obvious stopping places not far beyond would be relatively easy and not very long. Continuing to Calypso Cascades or Ouzel Falls makes a moderate length trip, while skiing all the way to Thunder Lake is a long and strenuous outing taking a full day.

About 15 miles south of Estes Park (1½ miles south of Meeker Park) and 3 miles north of Allens Park, on Rt. 7, one will see a sign for the Wild Basin Ranger Station. Turn west onto this road and drive past Copeland Lake to reach the National Park boundary after about ½ mile. In winter the road is blocked here by a gate. This is the starting point of the tour.

Head west along the road for 1¼ miles. One passes a turnoff to the right, crosses a bridge, goes along the south side of the stream and then crosses another bridge back to the north side of the stream and finally comes to the end of the road. At this point there is a large summer parking area that is at the Wild Basin trailhead.

At the southwest corner of the parking lot the trail begins near some signs, soon crosses small bridges and then climbs gradually as it goes along the north side of the stream and leads to Copeland Falls. For another ½ mile beyond this the trail wends its way over slabs and through the woods to a large bridge crossing to the south side of North St. Vrain Creek. After this the trail steepens noticably and at the 3¾ mile mark one arrives at a major trail junction and the Calypso Cascades. A shorter trip stops here before heading back.

To continue, turn right (west) past the cascades and cross a number of small bridges over the braided stream. The trail then zigzags up a steep slabby hill and levels off for a bit before another bridge is reached. Ouzel Falls can be seen from here, a short distance west through the forest. Continue following the trail as it stays fairly level for a while and starts curving to the left and passes a rocky point with good views back out the valley. Almost 1 mile beyond Ouzel Falls there is a turnoff to the left. This is the trail to Bluebird Lake. Soon after this, at the 5½ mile point of the tour, one crosses another large bridge over North St. Vrain Creek and then skis along its north side for the duration of the tour.

One mile past the bridge is a turnoff to the right. This is the trail to Lion Lakes. Stay on the main trail as it continues west, climbing gradually for another 1½ miles to Thunder Lake. To return to the car one simply skis back on out the trail. If the streambed is sufficiently snowed in it is pleasant to ski directly down this from Thunder Lake for a mile or two before rejoining the trail and following that for the rest of the return trip.

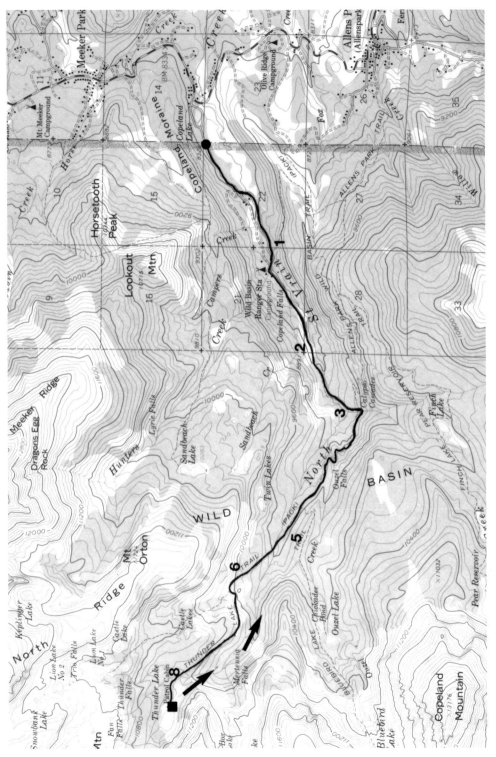

9 EAST INLET

Grade: Easy
Distance: 3 Miles—One Way
Elevation Change: 525 Feet
High Point: 9,100 Feet
Approximate Time: One-half Day
USGS Topographic Map:
  Shadow Mountain

Located on the western side of Rocky Mountain National Park this tour has a very different character than its counterparts on the eastern side. It receives and retains considerably more snow and is far less windy. Though rather a long way from the eastern slope its serene and beautiful setting make this a popular tour with local skiers.

Approach the East Inlet from the town of Grand Lake, 14 miles north of Granby, where one turns off to the east onto Rt. 278, the Grand Lake Village road. Drive along this for ⅓ of a mile and take a left at a fork in the road. This is marked by a sign for the Big Thompson Irrigation Tunnel. Drive for another 2½ miles around the northeast end of the lake to the parking area for the Adams Falls trailhead. This is near the west portal of the Adams Irrigation Tunnel.

Head southeast for about 200 yds. across the summer parking lot to signs, etc. at the start of the trail. The tour heads east on a good trail through the woods and soon crosses a bridge. Climb a steep hill to reach the top of a small rise. Near the top of this the trail turns sharply to the south for a short distance before heading east again. At a point a little less than ½ mile from the start a side trail goes off to the right to Adams Falls just to the south. Soon after this turnoff one reaches the National Park boundary and continues on to reach a big meadow. Skirt along the north edge of this meadow skiing in and out of the trees as the trail curves around, first to the left and then back to the right.

For another mile of almost level skiing the trail goes along near the edge of the meadows with occasional short rises and drops. At about the 2 mile mark one reaches the end of the meadows and the trail starts to climb. It is gradual at first as it passes some cliffs and a small side stream coming in from the north. Beyond a turnoff for a summer campsite it begins climbing more steeply. Continue steadily up, heading on a southeast course along the north side of the main valley. One can then go up to the left to reach a good viewpoint on a ridge or veer to the right a bit and contour along below a steep rise to reach the falls by simply following the stream.

To return to the car simply head back out one's tracks or if the meadows are covered with good snow ski straight out to the west across them.

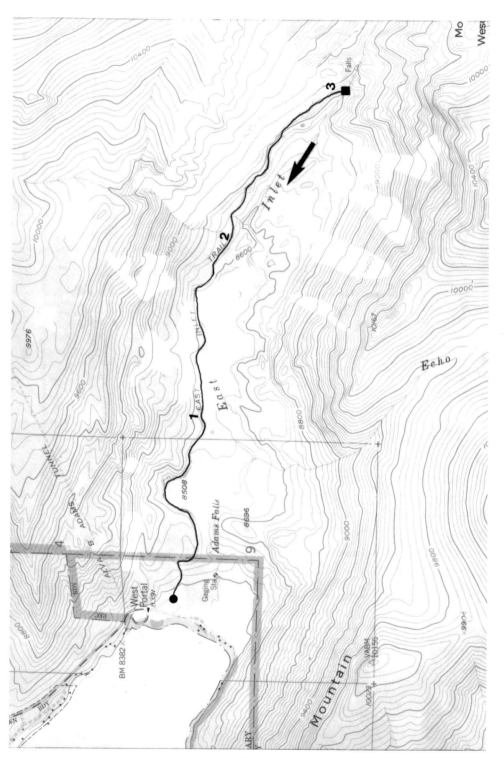

10 MIDDLE ST. VRAIN CREEK

Grade: Easy-Difficult
Distance: 10½ Miles—One Way
Elevation Change: 1,450 Feet
High Point: 10,900 Feet
Approximate Time: One Day
USGS Topographic Map:
  Allens Park
  Isolation Peak

This long gentle valley offers a relatively flat tour which follows jeep roads for most of its distance. The difficulty really only relates to the distance covered. Those seeking an easy tour can ski up the road a relatively short distance while those desiring a more demanding outing can continue up the valley. The further one goes the more spectacular the scenery becomes, and the glaciers at the head of the drainage, their cirques, and Elk Tooth are remote and wildly beautiful.

The tour all the way in to the glaciers covers a considerable distance and is quite strenuous. The lower part of the trip is forested, while the upper ½ of the tour crosses more open terrain. The head of the valley is at a deceptively high elevation and often windy and harsh conditions may occur. These as well as the remoteness of the valley terminus should be considered when planning this trip.

Drive along highway 72 to the Middle St. Vrain Campground. This is 5 miles south of the junction of Rt. 7 and Rt. 72. The campground is marked by signs and is on the outside (west) of a major U-turn, just to the west of Peaceful Valley. Park at a turnoff along the road, or if it is plowed, in a parking area just west of the highway.

Ski west from the parking area, through the campground and cross Middle St. Vrain Creek. Follow the road along the north side of the creek for ¾ of a mile then recross the stream to its south side. Traverse an open meadow, past a gaging station, and go through a wide gate as the road returns to the shelter of the trees. A slight climb is encountered over the next 2 miles then the road bears right and descends a little before turning west again and continuing on up the valley.

At this point, almost 3 miles from the start, a small trail turns off to the northeast, crosses the Middle St. Vrain creek, and heads back along the north side of the creek for ½ mile before rejoining the road. This is a good stopping point for those desiring a shorter tour. Either return to the start along the road or via a short loop on this trail.

The jeep road stays roughly parallel to the stream, climbing gradually as it continues west up the wooded valley. At about the 5 mile mark a side trail heads steeply back up to the left. Shortly beyond this the road descends slightly and crosses the stream and then continues for ½ mile more to a trail junction at the far end of a wind swept meadow. Here one finds trail signs as well as signs prohibiting further progress by motorized vehicles. The latter are usually ignored by snowmobiles who frequent this valley.

One more mile of gentle, almost flat skiing brings one to some old buildings on the north side of the creek. From here on the north side of the valley is rugged and precipitous. After another mile of skiing through woods and meadows the road fades out and one more or less follows the creek heading west up the drainage. Approximately 1½ mile of this brings one to the end of the trees and gradual open slopes below the spectacular south face of Elk Tooth. Turn southwest and head up steeper slopes to Lake Gibraltar at the entrance to a steep glaciated cirque.

The return trip out to the road follows the same route that one took coming in. It is somewhat quicker as one can follow their tracks and is slightly downhill the whole way.

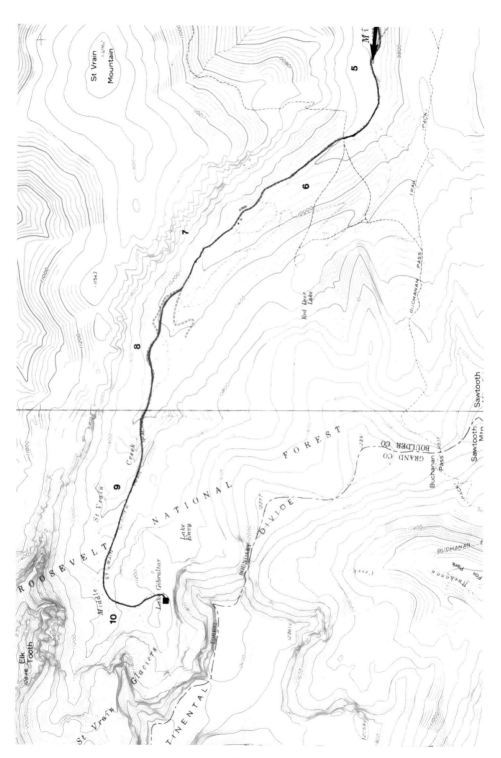

11 BRAINARD LAKE—NORTH TRAIL AND ROAD

Grade: Easy
Distance: 2½ Miles—One Way
Elevation Change: 320 Feet
High Point: 10,450 Feet
Approximate Time: One-half Day
USGS Topographic Map:
  Ward

The Brainard Lake area is undoubtedly one of the most popular and well known cross country ski areas in the entire Front Range. This trail and the following one more or less parallel the summer road into the lake and offer more sheltered alternatives to that approach. The North Trail provides a rolling and pleasant tour and is in the woods for most of its length. It can be used as the initial leg of a trip including tour #13—Blue Lake, or as a separate, shorter trip by itself. Due to the heavy use it is usually tracked and is well marked by signs and markers.

The approach is from Highway 72, just north of the turnoff to Ward. A paved road, well marked by signs, goes west from Rt. 72 toward Brainard Lake. Take this for 2½ miles to a point where the road is blocked by a gate. Park off the road along the last hundred yards or so.

The North Trail starts just past the gate, and is marked with trail signs. The first ¼ mile heads north, contouring around a ridge and climbing slightly. It then turns west and levels off, crossing the outlet stream from Red Rock Lake at the ½ mile mark. After one more mile of rolling up and down skiing one crosses South St. Vrain creek. Soon one reaches a wind swept meadow and after reentering the woods at its far side the trail starts climbing more steadily. At the 2 mile point it connects with the South St. Vrain trail.

Turn left (west) on this trail as it contours along a hillside before dropping down sharply to cross an open drainage. Ascend a short steep hill and continue west as the trail follows a vague, rising ridge for ½ mile. This wooded climb leads to an open and wind swept clearing. By going west, along the north edge of the clearing, one soon connects with the summer road just to the east of the parking lot for the Mitchell Lake-Blue Lake trail. To reach Brainard Lake itself, turn left on this road and follow it back to the lake. Alternatively, one can cross southwest, across the east end of the clearing and go slightly west along a low wooded rise to reach the CMC cabin. This is located just northwest of Brainard Lake and is maintained and operated by the CMC.

To return to the start of the tour one can either ski back out along the North Trail or, alternatively, ski out along the summer road. This is just to the south and circles Brainard Lake. From the east end of the lake it heads east for 2 miles, passing Red Rock Lakes, to the barricade blocking the road just west of where the cars were parked.

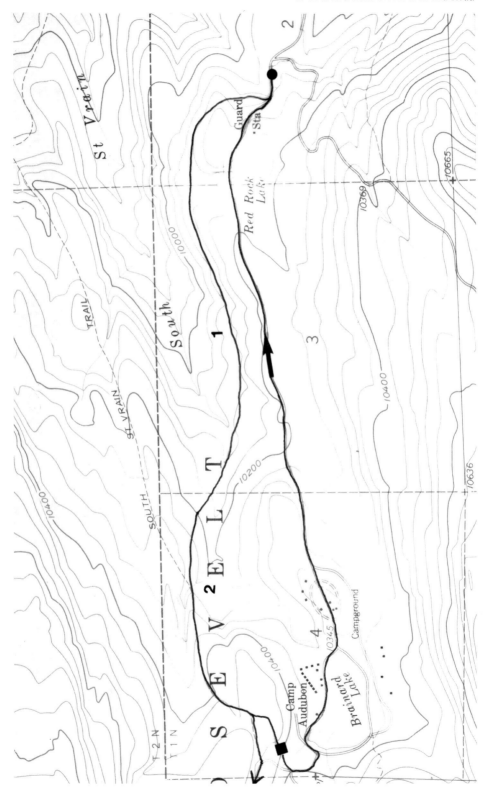

12 BRAINARD LAKE—SOUTH TRAIL AND ROAD

Grade: Easy
Distance: 2¼ Miles—One Way
Elevation Change: 360 Feet
High Point: 10,475 Feet
Approximate Time: One-half Day
USGS Topographic Map:
  Ward

Like the preceeding tour this trail offers a more pleasant alternative to the summer road as an approach to Brainard Lake. After the initial short uphill section the trail is essentially flat and parallels the road staying about ¼ mile south of it. It is well marked by ski trail signs and is a popular beginner's tour. Also it can be combined with a return along the road to make a short loop tour. The South Trail also provides

a good starting leg for skiers heading for Long Lake and Lake Isabelle (Tour #14).

The approach is from highway 72. Just north of the Ward turnoff a paved road, well marked by signs goes west from Rt. 72 toward Brainard Lake. Take this for 2½ miles until it is blocked by a gate. Park off the road along the last hundred yards or so.

Just beyond the barricade a well marked ski trail goes off to the left (south) side of the road. It begins with a fairly steep climb up a wide trail through the woods and after ¼ mile the angle of ascent becomes more gradual. Ski west along the trail which is well marked with blazes and signs as it traverses rolling terrain through the forest. After 1 mile large clearings open up off to the right but the trail stays just on the south edge of these.

As the trail continues the slight elevation gain is scarcely noticeable and after 2 miles one breaks out of the trees. Head to the northwest across an open meadow to connect with the summer road near the southwest corner of Brainard Lake.

To return to the car either ski back out along the South Trail or take the road on out. If one chooses the latter course, turn right along the road and take it to the east end of the lake. From there the road heads east for 2 miles, past Red Rock Lake, to the barricade blocking the road just to the west of where one parked.

30

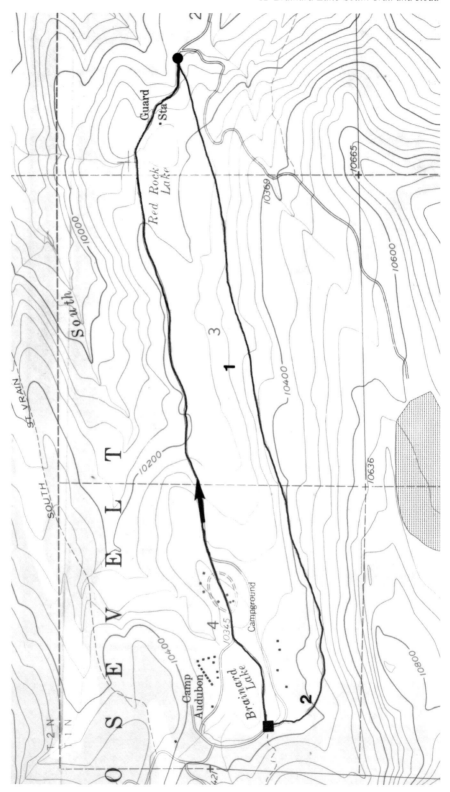

13 BLUE LAKE

Grade: Moderate
Distance: 5 Miles—One Way
Elevation Change: 900 Feet
High Point: 11,300 Feet
Approximate Time: One Day
USGS Topographic Map:
   Ward

Located to the west of Brainard Lake, Mitchell and Blue Lakes are situated in one of the most beautiful valleys in the Indian Peaks. Beyond Mitchell Lake this tour is above treeline and very exposed to the wind. However, the views of Mt. Toll, Paiute Peak, and Mt. Audubon are magnificent. Although the tour is fairly long the skiing itself is not very hard.

The most frequently used start to this tour is to ski into Brainard Lake via the North Trail (Tour #11). Beyond Brainard Lake follow the snow covered road to the parking lot at the Mitchell Lake-Blue Lake trailhead. At the west edge of this parking area is a large signboard with a rudimentary map and the start of the trail.

Ski west on the well marked trail through the forest. The trail climbs a little and then heads a bit to the left as it contours along the north side (south facing slope) of the Mitchell Lake stream drainage. Soon the terrain levels off. At a point about ¼ of a mile from the parking lot a bridge over the creek is crossed. Beyond this the trail swings left for a short distance and then curves back up to the right (northwest) as it climbs up a vague, wooded ridge and proceeds along the south side of the Mitchell Lake drainage. Soon the terrain levels off again and one leaves the woods, crosses meadows, and 1 mile from the parking lot one reaches Mitchell Lake.

Ski part way around the left (south) side of Mitchell Lake and up a drainage leading up to the southwest. Climb steeply at first but then, after ½ mile this levels off. One more mile of skiing across open meadows and up short steps following the drainage as it curves around to the west ensues. Head west up a long open valley and over a last short rise to reach Blue Lake.

The return trip follows one's ski tracks back to the parking lot. At this point either ski back out to the car along the North Trail or go on the Brainard Lake and follow the road on out.

32

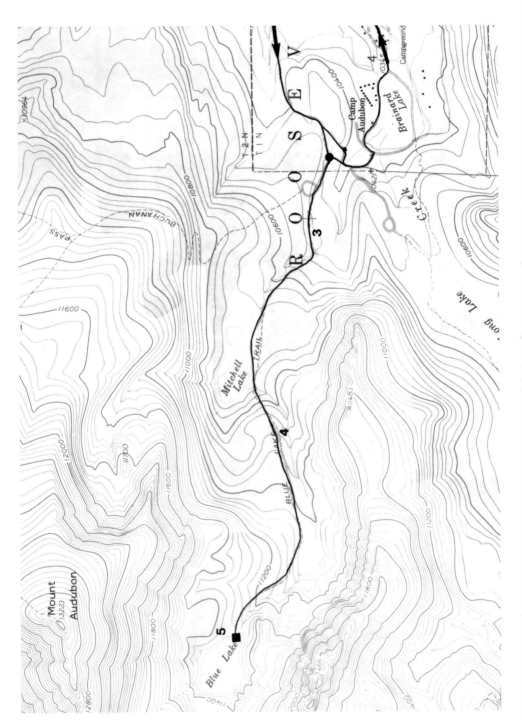

14 LAKE ISABELLE

Grade: Moderate
Distance: 4¾ Miles—One Way
Elevation Change: 500 Feet
High Point: 10,875 Feet
Approximate Time: One Day
USGS Topographic Map:
  Ward

As with the preceeding tour, this ski run really is a further continuation beyond Brainard Lake of one of the previously described trips to that point. It is described as starting at Brainard and leads up into the high mountain country of the Indian Peaks. Until the very last steep section it is near or below tree line, though on windy days it catches more than its share of the wind.

The most commonly used start to this trip is to take the South Trail (Tour #12) to Brainard Lake. From the west end of Brainard Lake ski west on the paved summer road toward the parking areas at the trailheads for Long Lake and Blue Lake. After a short distance on this road one turns left and follows a road to the parking area at the Long Lake trailhead. The trail starts at the southwest end of the parking lot and is marked with signs.

The first section is level though it is usually drifted badly by the wind. It heads to the southwest through some trees and very soon one comes to the northeast end of Long Lake. It is normally best to stay in or near the woods on the right side of the lake, especially if it is windy. Ski to the far end of Long Lake and continue on to the west, up an open and broad valley. Here again most parties tend to keep to the right side of the valley, near its edge.

One mile beyond Long Lake the valley is interrupted by a steep step. This is circumvented by climbing a steep snow filled gully heading up around its right (north) edge. Zigzag up the gully and near its top turn west again and climb over a low rise to reach Lake Isabelle. By continuing on up the gully and the drainage beyond instead of going to the lake one soon reaches a region of rolling ridges and bowls. The trail to Pawnee pass traverses these as it heads west and on up to the pass.

The return trip to the car simply reverses the course followed on the trip in. After a short and steep descent down the gully a long flat ski out to Long Lake is followed by the short wooded section back to the parking lot. Beyond this take the road and stay with that, past Brainard Lake, and then along it for 2 more miles to the east to reach the cars.

34

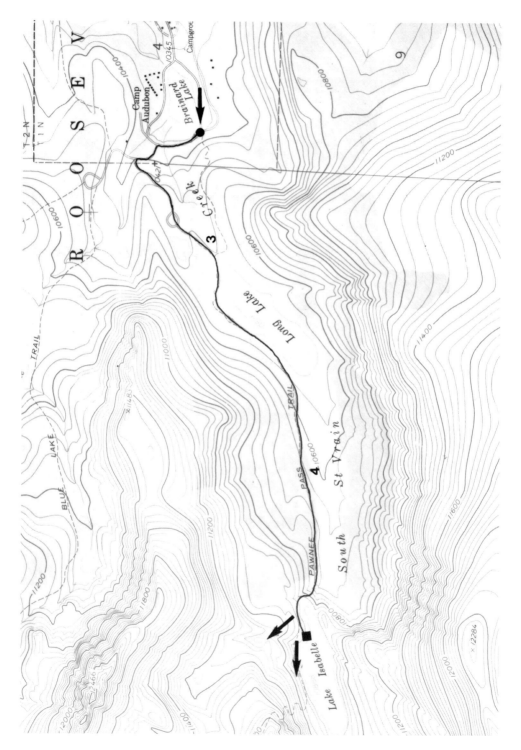

15 LEFT HAND RESERVOIR

Grade: Easy
Distance: 2 Miles—One Way
Elevation Change: 500 Feet
High Point: 10,620 Feet
Approximate Time: One-half Day
USGS Topographic Map:
   Ward

Just north of the Ward turnoff on highway 72 a road goes west toward Brainard Lake. This is well marked by signs. Drive west on this road for 2½ miles until the road is blocked by a barricade. Park along the road in the last section before the road is blocked.

Just down the road from the barricade a wide road heads off to the south. This is marked by signs indicating that it is the road to Left Hand Reservoir. Ski along this road as it climbs steadily and gradually for the first mile. The tour follows the road as it zigzags up a hill in this section and then crosses Left Hand Creek. Beyond that point the climb eases as the road continues through the forest.

After 1½ miles the road ends as one comes out into a big open meadow at the northeast end of the reservoir. Ski across the meadow to reach Left Hand Reservoir. One can stop here and ski around before heading back or continue on around the left side of the reservoir and on up to some big open slopes on the north side of Niwot Ridge. These often have good snow and are excellent places to practice one's downhill techniques.

Being short and quite easy this tour is one of the most popular beginning level ski tours in the Front Range. The trip follows a good summer road, the ascent is steady but gradual, and as most of the distance covered is in the trees it is a fairly sheltered run. In addition, the slopes of Niwot Ridge beyond the reservoir offer a good place for skiers to engage in some downhill runs.

The return back to the car is quick and straightforward. Simply ski back down the road which is often hardpacked and very fast. This leads back to the starting point in short order.

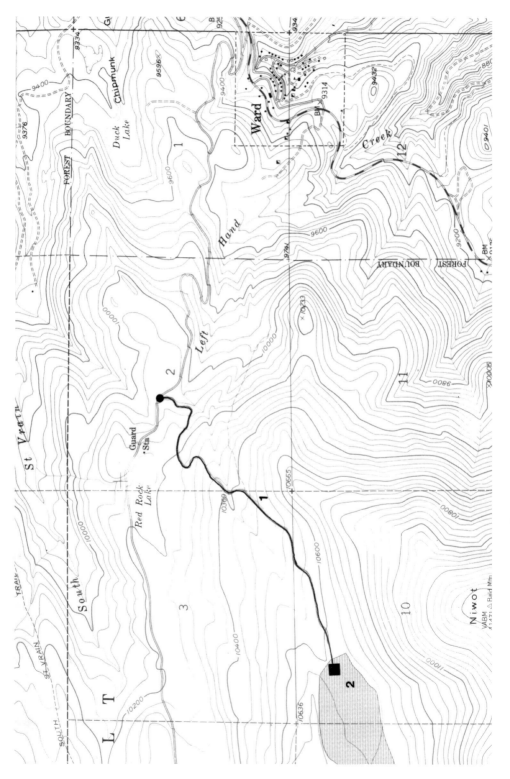

16 FOURTH OF JULY CAMPGROUND

Grade: Easy-Moderate
Distance: 5½ Miles—One Way
Elevation Change: 1,325 Feet
High Point: 10,125 Feet
Approximate Time: One Day
USGS Topographic Map:
  Nederland
  East Portal

In the summertime the Fourth of July campground is a popular camping and picnicing area as well as a major trailhead for numerous hikes and is readily accessible by automobile. In winter, however, the road is closed just west of the town of Eldora and it can only be reached by skiers and showshoers willing to undertake the fairly long approach. The touring is quite easy, following the road all the way. Sections are often windblown and bare but these can be skirted. The difficulty of the tour is related directly to the distance covered, so this can vary depending on how far one chooses to go. There are numerous private dwellings along the road and skiers should avoid these.

Just south of Nederland turn northwest off Rt. 72 onto a road marked by signs to the Lake Eldora Ski Area. Drive past the town high school and shortly beyond this is a road that forks off up to the left (south) to the Lake Eldora Ski Area. Do not take this but drive straight on and at the 4 mile mark pass through the old town of Eldora. The road continues west beyond the town but after a very short distance it is unplowed and impassable. Park here, being sure not to impede access to the private dwellings or not to block the road.

Start the tour by skiing west along the snow covered road. Pass a small rise and after about 1 mile one reaches a major fork. Stay to the right, along the main road, passing the left branch which leads down to the old townsight of Hessie. Continue along the gradually climbing road as it heads up the valley of the North Fork of Boulder Creek. The going is quite easy and the terrain fairly wooded. At the 2½ mile mark one passes some small turnoffs and cabins and soon thereafter passes through a meadow beyond which the road goes back into the woods.

Continue on along a northwesterly course through more of the same sort of countryside as the road maintains its steady but gradual climb. One skis on past Klondike Mountain, off to the right, and at the 4 mile point the road crosses a stream drainage coming down from the right. About ½ mile further things open up as one reaches a big clearing. Ski across this and past the picnic area to reach the Fourth of July campground which is in the trees beyond.

The return trip simply skis back down along one's tracks. The tracks and the steady grade of the descent make the return trip a good deal quicker and more enjoyable than coming in.

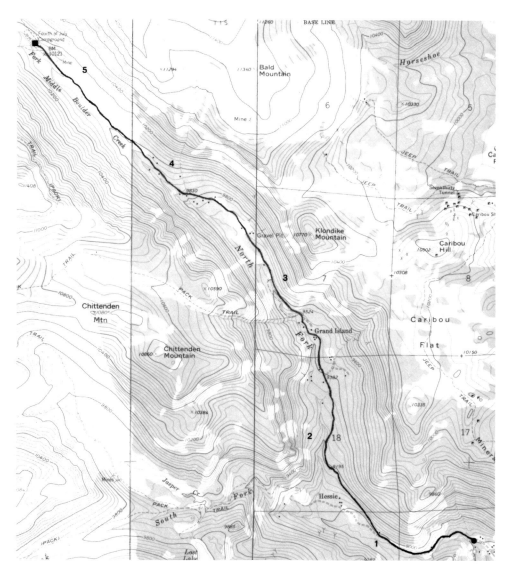

17 KING LAKE

Grade: Moderate-Difficult
Distance: 7½ Miles—One Way
Elevation Change: 1,680 Feet
High Point: 11,435 Feet
Approximate Time: One Day
USGS Topographic Map:
  Nederland
  East Portal

The long level trail to King Lake takes one into the far reaches of the eastern side of the Front Range. At the end of the tour the large bowls at the head of the valley are a very impressive sight. The relatively easy access from the Boulder-Denver region makes this entire area, and the various tours near here a popular weekend touring spot for Front Range skiers. Unfortunately the wind often causes much of the snow to be redistributed quickly and not always where skiers would like it to be.

The approach is by turning northwest off of Rt. 72 just south of Nederland onto a road marked by signs to the Lake Eldora Ski Area. Drive past the town high school and shortly beyond this a road forks left, heading up to the ski area. Do not take this left turn, but continue straight on the main road for 4 miles to the old town of Eldora. Drive through the town and very soon the road is unplowed and impassable. Park here, being careful not to impede access to private dwellings or not to block the road.

Start skiing west along the unplowed road. Go over a small rise and after 1 mile one reaches a fork in the road. The main road continues to the Fourth of July campground, but for this tour one takes the left hand branch which descends to the floor of the valley and the old townsight of Hessie. Ski through the old town sight and cross the creek.

Beyond this the road/trail zigzags up an open hillside then continues uphill through woods. Soon the jeep road levels off and crosses another creek. Just past the 2 mile point one crosses Lost Lake Creek and heads out into a big open area. Near the west end of this clearing, about 2½ miles from the start of the tour, the Lost Lake trail heads off to the left (south). Continue a short distance west and arrive at another fork in the road. The right (north) fork goes up Jasper Creek. Take the left (south) fork which is marked with signs for King Lake and head west on this as the trail proceeds along the north side of the creek. One skis back into the forest as the trail climbs slightly for the next ½ mile to reach another clearing. After 2 more miles of gradual skiing either along the trail or up the creekbed itself the jeep trail crosses to the south side of the creek (South Fork of Middle Boulder Creek).

Another 1½ miles of easy skiing keeps following the stream west to steep slopes which form a sort of step below King Lake. Head up to the northwest and climb lower angled slopes to a level area. Turn left, back to the southwest for a short way to reach King Lake.

The descent simply retraces the route down the gradual drainage out to the east. An alternative to skiing along the jeep trail is to ski out along the streambed itself, and as this often holds more snow it may offer better skiing.

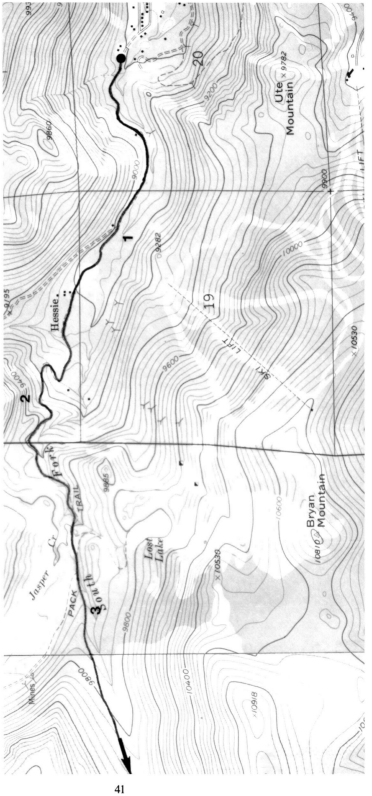

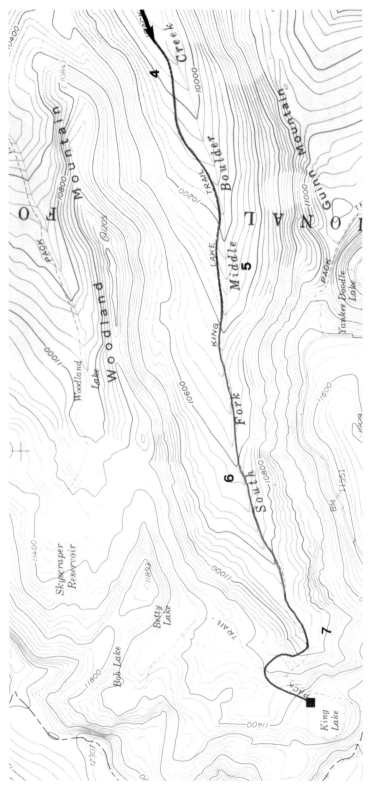

18 LOST LAKE

Grade: Easy
Distance: 3 Miles—One Way
Elevation Change: 990 Feet
High Point: 9,790 Feet
Approximate Time: One-half Day
USGS Topographic Map:
Nederland

This is a short and popular tour, frequently used by beginning skiers seeking a nearby trip that leads to a high mountain lake. The scenery is pleasant and the skiing not difficult. The tour is the same as #17—King Lake-for the first 2½ miles. Beyond that point a short section of moderately steep uphill leads to the lake itself.

Approach by turning off of Rt. 72 just south of Nederland onto the road marked by signs for the Lake Eldora Ski Area. Drive past the high school and continue west, past the road which forks off to the left and goes up to the ski area. After 4 miles one reaches the old town of Eldora and continues through it. Just a short distance west of Eldora the road is unplowed and impassable. Park here being careful not to impede access to private drives or to block the road.

Start skiing west along the unplowed road. Go over a small rise and after 1 mile one comes to a major fork in the road. Take the turnoff which veers left and which descends to the valley floor and soon brings one to the old Hessie town sight. Ski through this past several old buildings and cross the stream a short distance further west. Beyond this the jeep trail zigzags up a steep hillside and then reenters the woods. The terrain gradually levels off and just over 2 miles from the start one crosses another creek and arrives at a large, open clearing. Head across this to reach the trail junction which is well marked by signs.

The trail to Lost Lake turns off here, heading south as it starts the short steep climb to the lake. At first the trail heads a bit to the right but soon swings back to the left as it ascends the hillside. After ½ mile of climbing one comes to Lost Lake.

The return trip can follow the jeep trail back down from the lake, reversing one's ascent route. It is often better to simply ski down the drainage from Lost Lake for the first ½ mile of the return trip. This frequently has much better snow and brings one directly down to the meadow where one turned off from the King Lake trail. Head east along this trail to return to the trailhead.

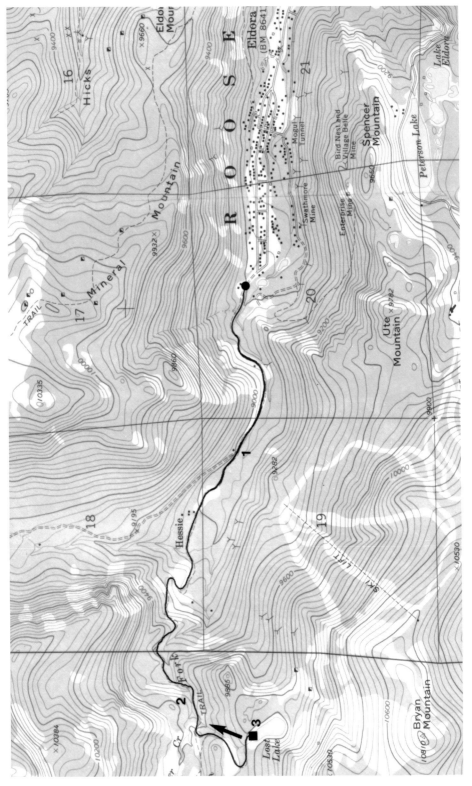

19 JENNY CREEK

Grade: Moderate-Difficult
Distance: 5½ Miles—One Way
Elevation Change: 1,330 Feet
High Point: 10,715 Feet
Approximate Time: One Day
USGS Topographic Map:
  Nederland
  East Portal

One of the real classic Front Range ski tours, this long pleasant trip is an old favorite with many skiers. Most of the distance covered is in the trees and sheltered from the wind to a large degree. The first part of the course is commonly shared with a number of nearby trips. The access trail to Jenny Creek is well marked and once in the creek drainage this trip follows a prominent jeep trail. The initial part of the tour crosses private land, the Lake Eldora Ski Area, and so one should be careful to stay on the public access trail provided.

Start the tour at the Lake Eldora Ski Area. This is reached by turning off of Rt. 72 just south of Nederland. The turnoff is well marked by signs for the ski area. Drive west past the high school and 1¼ miles from the turnoff one reaches a side road that turns off to the left, heading up to the ski area. Turn onto this and wind up a long hill and then as the road levels off pass Peterson Lake. A short distance further turn left into the large parking lot at the base of the Ho Hum lift, servicing the beginner ski run just to the south of the parking area. Also there is a small building here which is the ticket booth for the Lake Eldora Ski Area touring facilities.

Start skiing at the lower left corner of the downhill run near a sign indicating the forest access trail. Climb up to the upper right corner of the slope and then go west, along the south edge of the ski runs. Follow the forest access trail signs and start through the trees and cross a small rise. Cross a small dip and then go up again toward the southwest as the trail veers away from the downhill runs, and continues through the trees, dropping a bit at first but then once again climbing steadily. After 1 mile the trail levels off a bit and comes to a wide swath in the forest and heads south. Ski down this a short way and then turn sharply right on a narrower trail that begins a long and steady descent to the west. This slants all the way down the hillside and intersects the Jenny Creek trail near the bottom of the valley.

Now ski west up the jeep trail. This climbs gradually and after ¼ of a mile the trail to Guinn Mountain veers off up to the right. Keep going straight ahead on the jeep trail which stays just north of Jenny Creek. It is a short distance above the creekbed and runs along the south-facing hillside. At about the 4 mile point the trail steepens noticeably as one starts to pass around the south side of Guinn Mountain. The next mile continues along in the trees gradually curving to the northwest as the trail curls around the base of the mountain. At this point one emerges from the forest and ½ mile more of skiing up open meadows, climbing several short rises, brings one to Yankee Doodle Lake.

The descent returns along the same trail. As it is downhill for a long way it goes much more quickly than the trip in. One should take care not to miss the turnoff on the north side of the trail that leads back up the hillside on the forest access trail to the ski area. The turnoff is marked with signs and quite obvious if one is looking for it.

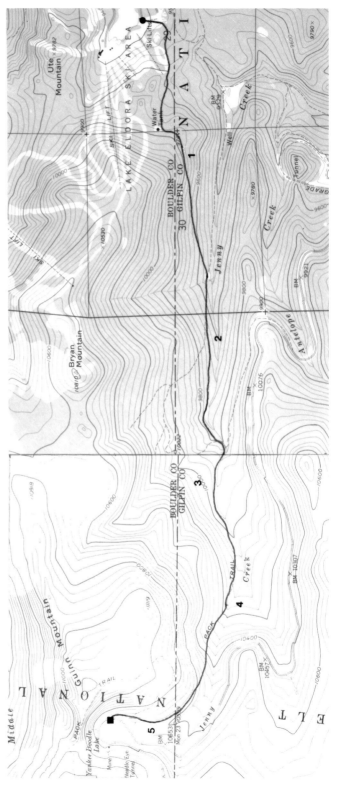

20 ANTELOPE RIDGE

Grade: Easy
Distance: 7½ Miles—Round Trip
Elevation Change: 620 Feet
High Point: 9,890 Feet
Approximate Time: One-half Day
USGS Topographic Map:
Nederland

The Antelope Ridge tour is often overlooked by skiers using the area behind Lake Eldora Ski Area. A step up in difficulty from the nearby commercial touring trails it is still quite a bit less strenuous than the other tours described near here. The one real complication is that the easterly portion of the trip overlaps some of the trails maintained by the ski area for their commercial touring area. A fee is charged for the use of these trails.

Nevertheless, the gradual uphill and downhill stretches of this trip and the delightful forests along Jenny Creek and Antelope Ridge make the tour very enjoyable and a good one for beginners desiring to extend their parameters a bit.

Start the tour at the Lake Eldora Ski Area. This is reached by turning off Rt. 72 just south of Nederland. The turnoff is well marked by signs for the ski area. Drive west past the high school and 1¼ miles from the turnoff one reaches a side road that turns off to the left, heading up to the ski area. Turn onto this and wind up a long hill and then as the road levels off pass Peterson Lake. A short distance further turn left into the large parking lot at the base of the Ho Hum lift, servicing the beginner ski run just to the south of the parking area. Also there is a small building here which is the ticket booth for the Lake Eldora Ski Area touring facilities.

Start skiing at the lower left corner of the downhill run near a sign indicating the forest access trail. Climb up to the upper right corner of the slope and then go west, along the south edge of the ski runs. Follow the forest access trail signs and start through the woods and cross a small rise. Cross a small dip and then go up again toward the southwest as the trail veers away from the downhill runs. Continue through

the trees, dropping at first but then once again climbing steadily. After 1 mile the trail levels off a bit and comes to a wide swath in the forest that runs off to the south. Ski down this a short way and then turn sharply to the right on a narrower trail that begins a long and steady descent to the west. This slants all the way down the hillside and intersects the Jenny Creek trail near the bottom of the valley.

Ski west up the jeep trail which climbs gradually and after ¼ of a mile pass the trail to Guinn Mountain which heads up to the right. Keep going straight ahead on the main trail for almost another ½ mile. At this point one should take a turnoff to the left on a small trail that heads down a short, steep drop to Jenny Creek. Cross to the south side of the creek and then the trail turns sharply to the left (southeast) and angles back up the hillside on the south side of the creek.

For ½ mile one climbs steadily up the north facing hillside of Antelope Ridge. At the crest of the ridge the trail curves back to the southwest and one descends a short distance and passes a cable across the trail. Be careful not to come up on this obstacle too quickly. As the trail continues down toward the southwest one very soon comes to a small trail heading off sharply back to the left (east) at a point which is only a few hundred yards from the crest of the ridge.

Take this turnoff which descends steadily along the wooded south-facing hillside of the ridge. About ½ way down one passes some old mine buildings which are off on the right, on the south side of Antelope Creek. A mile of fast downhill skiing leads to a trail junction at which one turns left and continues on down to the Jenny Creek Drainage. Go left here, heading north, up along the west side of the creek. Eventually cross to the east side of the creek and up along good trails to a big open meadow.

At this point one has two options. The first is to ski west, back up along Jenny Creek for 1¼ miles to intersect the forest access trail and take that back to the ski area. The second, and shorter, option is to head northeast on the maintained trails, up a long, curving draw that climbs steadily and leads to a 4 way intersection. Turn left at this trail junction and ski a short way to the north and east to reach the top of the Ho Hum lift.

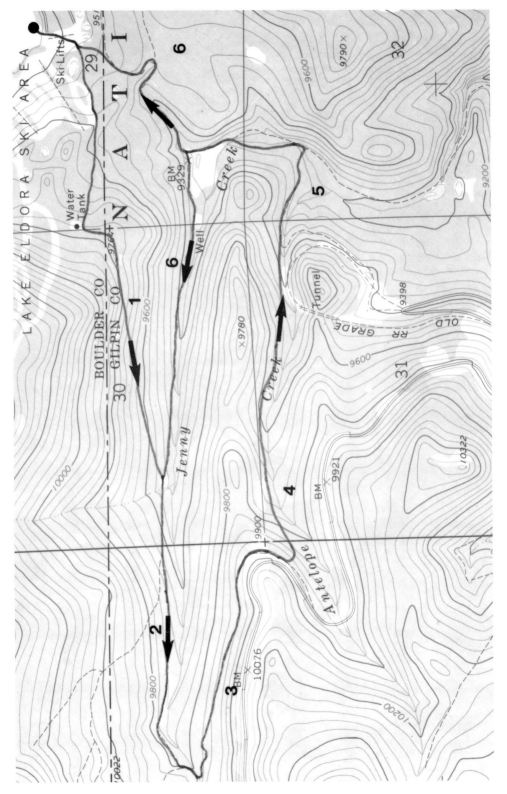

21 GUINN MOUNTAIN

Grade: Difficult
Distance: 5 Miles—One Way
Elevation Change: 1,560 Feet
High Point: 11,200 Feet
Approximate Time: One Day
USGS Topographic Map:
  Nederland
  East Portal

The tour up Guinn Mountain is one of the tried and true classics of Front Range skiing. Relatively few parties actually go all the way to the windblown top of the peak. Instead most skiers prefer to stop at the Arestua hut a short distance below. This cabin was erected by the Colorado Mountain Club and is maintained by them. Proper care and usage is requested to keep it as it is. For years this cabin has been a popular goal for cross-country skiers and the long strenuous climb up is rewarded by a stop for lunch at this cozy haven. The descent, often overlooked during the ascent, is steep and fast and the narrow trail through the woods often is a mass of holes in the snow caused by crashing skiers. In addition this tour is the first leg of the Rollins Pass tour (#22) and contains almost all of the strenuous uphill portion of that trip. During the winter of 1982-83 the trail to the hut was remarked with numerous diamond shaped blue markers. This has made the route finding, especially in the upper parts, a good deal easier.

Start at the Lake Eldora Ski Area. This is reached by turning off Rt. 72 just south of Nederland. The turnoff is well marked by signs for the ski area. Drive west past the high school and 1¼ miles from the turnoff one reaches a side road that turns off to the left, heading up to the ski area. Turn onto this and wind up a long hill and then as the road levels off pass Peterson Lake. A short distance further turn left into the large parking lot at the base of the Ho Hum lift, servicing the beginners ski run just to the south of the parking area. Also there is a small building here which is the ticket booth for the Lake Eldora Ski Area touring facilities.

Start skiing at the lower left corner of the downhill run near a sign indicating the forest access trail. Climb up to the upper right corner of the slope and then go west, along the south edge of the ski runs. Follow the forest access trail signs and start through the woods and cross a small rise. Cross a small dip and then go up again toward the southwest as the trail veers away from the downhill runs. Continue through the trees, dropping at first but then once again climbing steadily. After 1 mile the trail levels off a bit and comes to a wide swath running south through the forest. Ski down this a short way and then turn sharply to the right on a narrower trail that begins a long and steady descent to the west. This slants all the way down the hillside and intersects the Jenny Creek trail near the bottom of the valley.

Ski west up the jeep trail which climbs steadily and after ¼ mile a trail cuts off up to the right. This is the Guinn Mountain trail and climbs steadily to the northwest for ½ mile then

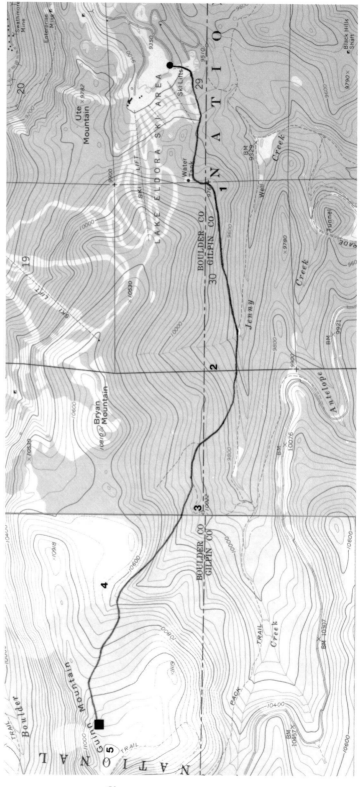

turns left and levels off for a while. After ¼ mile it begins climbing steeply once again up through a pine forest. Gradually the angle eases as the trail curves along the southwest facing hillside. At the 3½ mile point one comes to an open ravine with a ruined cabin on its right side. Continue up the drainage and zigzag up the steep slopes at its upper end.

At the upper left corner of these slopes the trail heads back into the woods. The next section is fairly level and heavily wooded. Unless a trail has been broken the best route through the remaining 1½ miles can be hard to find. Basically one heads west following a winding trail sporadically marked by an assortment of blazes, flags, and markers. The trail passes an old log structure and crosses through several small clearings as it leads through these forests. Eventually (after 1¼ miles) one breaks out of the woods into a wide opening that runs east-west. This was created when a pipeline was laid across the mountains. The Arestua hut is located a couple of hundred yards west along this clearing. It faces east and is on the left (south) side of the clearing, nestled in a clump of trees.

To reach the top of Guinn Mountain from the hut just continue west, up the pipe line clearings which lead directly to the open and wind swept summit. The fastest and surest descent is to ski back down following the same route used to reach the hut. The trip down the trail is very steep and narrow in sections but soon brings one down to the gentle trail of Jenny Creek. Head down this and then out along the forest access trail to return to the ski area.

22 ROLLINS PASS

Grade: Difficult
Distance: 16½ Miles—One Way Trip
Elevation Change: 2,291 Feet, With a
**   296 Foot Loss in an East-West Direction**
High Point: 11,671 Feet
Approximate Time: One or Two Days
USGS Topographic Map:
**   Nederland**
**   East Portal**
**   Fraser**

This is certainly the most pleasant and most popular of the trans-Front Range tours. The trip is described as going in an east to west direction because it is almost always done this way. This is for logistical reasons; most skiers will be starting from the eastern slope. Also in this direction there is actually a total net loss of elevation and most of the climbing is done early in the tour and a very large part of the distance is downhill when done going from east to west. After the initial steep climb up to Guinn Mountain the tour follows the old railroad bed west on a long gradual ascent to Rollins Pass. This section is all above the trees and in good weather the scenery is breathtaking. It is very exposed and high winds are very common. In the event of bad weather it is advisable to turn back at Guinn Mountain, as beyond this point the degree of seriousness increases greatly.

The middle part of the tour, across the divide itself, is frequently bare and it is often necessary to walk a lot of it. On the western side of the range more snow is usually encountered and from Rollins Pass west the tour is almost all downhill and goes fairly quickly. The trip can reasonably be done in one very long day but some parties prefer to take advantage of the Arestua hut and spend the night there en route. As the trip starts at the Lake Eldora Ski Area and ends at the Winter Park Ski Area one must take into consideration some means of return. Many parties like to arrange to be picked up at Winter Park thus avoiding any problems with the return trip.

Start at the Lake Eldora Ski Area and ski to the Arestua hut on Guinn Mountain. For the approach to the ski area and a description of the route to this hut refer to tour #21. The remainder of the trip is described from this point on.

From the hut ski west up the pipeline clearings to reach the summit of Guinn Mountain. Directly to the west one can see the old railroad grade. Ski down an open swath studded with tree stumps which leads west to a saddle on the ridgeline. Beyond this a short and steep open hillside is ascended to reach the old road bed. Turn right and go along the road and very shortly one curves left (west) again and heads along a very steep north facing hillside. Soon one comes to the old trestles. Just before these the road is often buried and it may be necessary to cross a very steep and narrow snow chute which requires

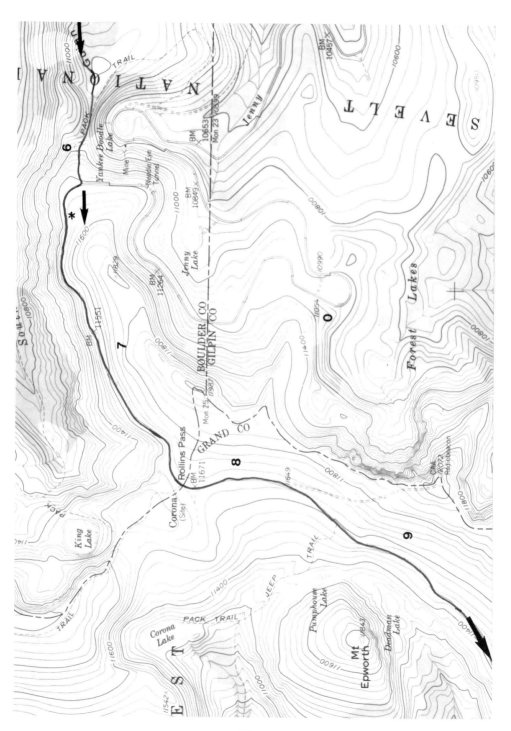

55

great care. If this is too risky one can backtrack a little and climb up to the south onto a broad rocky plateau and walk along parallel to the road for 1 mile to bypass this section. As the road bed heads west it crosses several trestles in the next 2 miles. The section through here is very exposed and spectacular and unquestionalby is the most exciting part of the trip. Gradually the grade leads up to Rollins Pass, at which one gets fantastic views of almost the entire Front Range.

From the pass the road heads southwest and gradually descends as it traverses the gentle open hillside. One should resist the temptation at this point to descend to the west into the Ranch Creek drainage but should stay with the road instead. The road is usually very obvious and often wind blown in places as well as being intermittantly marked by posts. After ¾ of a mile a fork goes off to the left up to a radio beacon. Keep on skiing down to the southwest along the road and after another 2½ miles pass the project study area. For 1 more mile the road curves on and finally comes to Riflesight Notch. This narrow gap in the ridge is spanned by a large wooden trestle which is visible for miles. At Riflesight Notch the tour leaves the old road bed and heads south, directly down a narrow and steep drainage. One mile of steep downhill skiing brings one to the base of this and out into the South Fork of Ranch Creek valley. Turn west and ski a short distance down the valley to rejoin the road bed.

Continue to the west along the road for 1 mile until it passes through a low gap in the ridge and ski by the low hill off to the right. Below and to the left is the upper end of the Buck Creek drainage. Head down into this, which is steep and heavily wooded at first. As one descends to the southwest in this valley an open clearing along the creek is soon reached. Cross to the far left corner of this clearing and on the hillside to the left of the creek locate an old road or logging trail. This winds steeply down the valley, staying to the left of Buck Creek all the way. This leads out to the Arrow Aquaduct road. Turn left along this and ski or walk a short way until one reaches a steep cut through the trees directly above the ski area. Either ski down this to highway 40 and the Winter Park Ski Area or continue a very short distance further along the road to reach the highway.

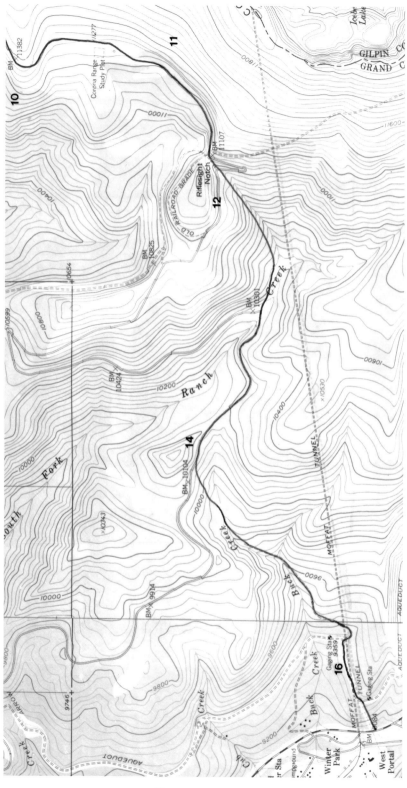

23 JENNY LIND GULCH

Grade: Easy
Distance: 2 Miles—One Way
Elevation Change: 1,390 Feet
High Point: 10,190 Feet
Approximate Time: One-half Day
USGS Topographic Map:
Nederland

The relatively close proximity of this tour to major population centers and its pleasant, easy skiing makes this tour attractive to many skiers. Once across the initial meadow, which is often very windy, the tour is in the trees much of the way and fairly sheltered. When snow conditions are good the big open slopes at the upper end of the tour are a fine spot for beginning skiers to practice some downhill runs. In past years the weekend crowds have resulted in parking problems. One should be careful not to block the road and not to park in any areas where it is indicated not to do so.

Take Rt. 72/119 to Rollinsville. From this small town head west on a good dirt road that leads to Tolland and the East Portal. Drive along this road for 4¼ miles at which point one will see a fence with a gate off on the south side of the road. Park here. As a point of reference this is also 1 mile before the town of Tolland.

Start skiing on the south side of the road and cross a short meadow to reach the gate in the fence. Go through this and ski south following an old mining road. Very soon the road divides. The left branch goes off onto private property.

Take the right hand fork of the road and ski straight ahead on this as it goes in and out of some trees, staying on the east side of a small creek. Soon the trail crosses to the west side of the creek and goes along this for a mile, passing some old mine sites up on the hillside to the east.

After about 1 mile the trail crosses a side stream that comes in from the right (west). From this point on the grade steepens slightly as the tour continues straight on up the valley. Proceed for most of another mile up the somewhat wooded valley. Eventually the trail emerges from the trees into a region of open hillsides covered with scattered tree stumps. Head on up these to reach the far point of the trip.

Here one is faced with a choice of 2 return routes. The simplest and easiest is to turn around and ski back the way one came in. This is quite fast and straightforward. The first ½ of this route is moderately steep and quite exciting, while the last ½ is more gradual. Those preferring a somewhat longer and more adventurous route can take the following line of return. Climb the open hillside up to the right (southwest) for several hundred feet. This brings one up onto a broad ridge. Contour around this to the northwest and then go down slightly to the west into the head of a drainage that leads down to the northeast. Ski down this valley and descend along the northwest side of the creek. Here one can pick up a mining road trail that parallels the creek and leads on down the drainage until it rejoins the main valley of Jenny Lind Gulch. Turn left (north) and ski out the main trail for a mile to reach the car.

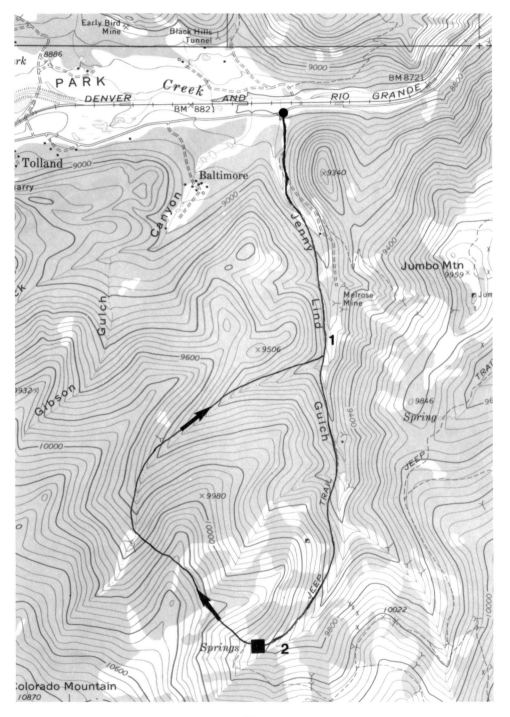

24 FOREST LAKES

Grade: Difficult
Distance: 4 Miles—One Way
Elevation Change: 1,610 Feet
High Point: 10,820 Feet
Approximate Time: One-half Day
USGS Topographic Map:
  East Portal

The high and secluded Forest Lakes cirque is often bypassed by skiers in favor of the better known Rogers Pass area tour. It is not an especially long tour in terms of the distance covered but it does involve a rather steep and substantial ascent. In recent years the access to this area, as with any of the trips originating from the East Portal, has become a problem. At the time of this writing this has not been clarified or resolved.

The access crosses private land and for many years this was permitted without problems. However, in 1979-80 a private club leased the property involved and temporarily closed off the access to the National Forest land beyond. Eventually they began charging a fee for skiing on the private land and imposed this on both skiers planning to ski on the property or simply crossing it en route to the public lands. At that time the Forest Service and the CMC began planning an alternative access route. By 1982-83 the fees were not being imposed, no alternate access had been established and the entire matter was in an unresolved mess.

Since this tour, as well as the next three, all are rather old and traditional Front Range ski tours they have been included in this book. This has been done for the sake of completeness and to keep this information available. In addition it is hoped that before too long the problems will be resolved and that ski tourers and hikers will again be allowed access to these recreation areas of our National Forest lands. Those seeking more recent information on the status of this matter are advised to contact the CMC or the offices of the Roosevelt National Forest.

To reach the start of the tour take Rt. 119 to Rollinsville. Turn west onto a dirt road marked by signs for Tolland and East Portal. Drive 8½ miles west on this road to its terminus at a large group of buildings at the East Portal of the Moffat Tunnel. These facilities and the nearby property are owned by the railroad and one should carefully observe and respect the regulations and parking situation. From the parking area head south across a bridge and pass a metal gate. Then continue southwest across a meadow to the trailhead. This is at a gate in a wooden fence by a small building at the edge of the woods.

Start skiing up a rough road or trail that starts out being almost flat and goes through the woods and passes several private buildings. After ½ mile one crosses a small meadow and then reenters the trees. Now the trail climbs a little more steeply as it continues for another ½ mile, crossing a small stream. At the 1 mile mark it reaches a huge open clearing with some old ruined buildings.

At the near (northeast) end of the meadow turn sharply to the right and climb a short way up the open slope. The trail to Forest Lakes doubles back at this point, leaving the main trail and heading northeast as it slants up the steep south facing side of the valley for ½ mile until it crosses Arapahoe Creek. Beyond the creek the trail climbs very steeply for a short distance and then curves to the left. It then runs parallel to the creek and climbs steadily for the next mile. This section is usually well flagged and brings one to a small meadow below a steep wooded hillside. Cross the meadow and angle up a little to the right (north) as one climbs the steep hillside heading northwesterly. One can either follow the stream bed up this section or ski through the woods nearby. As the angle eases off follow the creek on up to the lower Forest Lake. Cross the lake to its northwest end and continue on up the drainage through several meadows and up some short steep sections. After ½ mile one crosses over a low rise to reach the upper Forest Lake.

In descent merely ski down the drainage or retrace one's tracks to reach the small meadow below the steep wooded hillside. From there ski back down along the trail to the starting point.

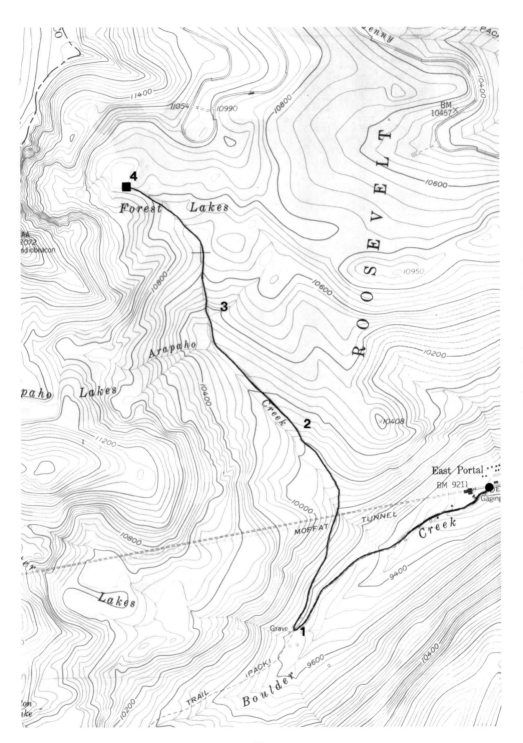

25 LITTLE HAUTE ROUTE

Grade: Difficult
Distance: 12½ Miles—One Way Trip
Elevation Change: 1,820 Feet, 150 Foot Loss
High Point: 11,030 Feet
Approximate Time: One Day
USGS Topographic Map:
  Nederland
  East Portal

The rather glamorous sounding name derives from a famous ski trip in the Alps. While hardly a fair comparison, this delightful and long trip does offer the skier a tour through relatively remote terrain in the beautiful higher regions of this part of the Front Range. As described here the trip starts at the East Portal and ends at the Lake Eldora Ski Area. Therefore return transportation must be planned. For most of the trip one is below timberline and after the initial climbing to Forest Lakes the remainder of the distance is largely downhill.

This is really a combination of two other tours, #24—Forest Lakes and #19—Jenny Creek with a short connecting section between them. The open section above Yankee Doodle Lake is often subject to high winds and conditions there can be quite severe. On a good day, with good snow conditions and weather the views and relaxed nature of the skiing make this one of the finest trips on the eastern side of the divide.

Unfortunately the access problems at the East Portal are currently unresolved and so the initial part of this trip is restricted. For a fuller explanation of this matter refer to the discussion in the description of the Forest Lake Tour (#24). The approach and first part of the trip correspond with the Forest Lake trip as well and that description should be used for the first part of this tour; this description begins at the upper Forest Lake.

From the lake head northeast. This involves climbing up a wooded hillside for ⅓ of a mile to the top of a low ridge. Cross to the north side of the rise and soon one will intersect the Rollins Pass road. At this point the road is at the southern apex of a huge hairpin loop. Turn to the right on the road and follow it as it curves around on a convoluted course. At first one goes east, then back north, east once again, and then north, northwest, and northeast as the road slowly contours down the hillside. Basically in this section one is heading in a northeasterly direction. After 1 mile one crosses the outlet from Jenny Lake (located up to the left). Ski on along the road heading northeast for ¼ mile more, at which point one is just to the south of Yankee Doodle Lake.

Descend directly east, crossing the road again lower down, to reach the bottom of the Jenny Creek valley. Cross the creek and ski up along its northeast side to pick up the Jenny Creek trail which is running parallel to the creek, below the base of Guinn Mountain. The exact point at which one chooses to make this short jaunt will vary. On good days one may prefer to go all the way to Yankee Doodle Lake before heading down the valley, while in adverse conditions one may choose to head more directly down.

In any event once the trail is located this is followed on out to the east to the ski area. It is about 5 miles to the forest access trail turnoff. This is well marked and on the left (north) side of the trail. This leads up the north side of the valley to the ski area. Those desiring more details of this last part of the tour should refer to the description for the Jenny Creek tour (#19).

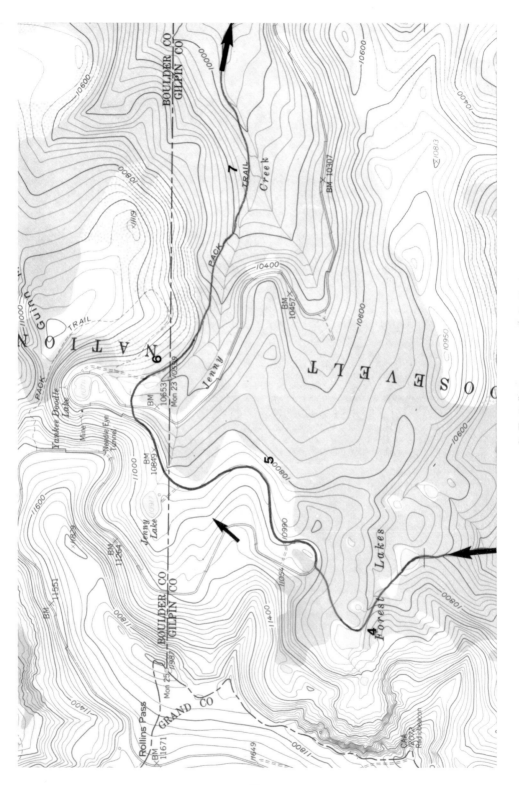

26 ROGERS PASS LAKE

Grade: Difficult
Distance: 4½ Miles—One Way
Elevation Change: 2,000 Feet
High Point: 11,130 Feet
Approximate Time: One Day
USGS Topographic Map:
  East Portal
  Empire

As with the preceeding two routes the initial part of this tour crosses private land and access is currently restricted. Please refer to the description for tour #24—Forest Lakes for a further explanation of this situation. The tour to Rogers Pass Lake is another old favorite. In past years the return trip down the steep and narrow trail has been responsible for many progressing skiers to have second thoughts about continuing with the sport. The CMC has established a small domed hut on the rise to the east of the lake and that has been a popular goal for day skiers as well as providing a convenient shelter for overnight use.

Rogers Pass Lake is situated high in a spectacular alpine cirque and very often it is mistakenly referred to as Heart Lake, which is located nearby. The tour itself is quite steep and strenuous and the descent very fast and often more trying than the ascent.

Take Rt. 119 to Rollinsville and turn west onto a dirt road marked with signs for Tolland and East Portal. Drive 8½ miles west on this road to its terminus at a group of buildings at the east portal of the Moffat Tunnel. This complex is all property of the railroad and one should carefully observe and respect the parking situation. Head south across a bridge and pass a metal gate. Then go southwest across a meadow to the trailhead. This is at a gate in a fence by a small building at the edge of the woods.

Start skiing up a trail or rough road that is almost level and goes through the woods passing several private buildings. After ½ mile one crosses a small meadow and then reenters the forest. Now the trail climbs a bit more as it continues for another ½ mile, crossing a small stream and at the 1 mile mark it reaches a huge open clearing with some ruined buildings. Ski straight ahead across this clearing to its far end.

At the far right (upper) corner of the clearing the trail reenters the woods and begins climbing very steeply. For the next mile the narrow trail ascends continuously along the hillside to the right of a stream. About ½ way along one passes a turnoff on the right that is the summer trail to Crater Lakes. As the angle lessens the trail turns south, paralleling South Boulder Creek and winds through the trees staying on the west side of the creek. After ½ mile the climb steepens again and one can either stay with the trail, which may be somewhat difficult to follow exactly if not tracked, or follow the bed of the creek itself. This section gives way in turn to a series of less steep clearings and short rises as one nears the tree line. Ski out of the woods and cross a series of open meadows to finally reach Rogers Pass Lake.

The Pfiffner Hut is located a couple hundred yards east of the lake and is on the north side of the creek drainage. It is a low domed structure and as it is nestled down in a small clump of trees it is often difficult to locate. The wild and rapid descent returns down the ski tracks and trail to the start. Sometimes parties prefer to follow the streambed for part of the descent to avoid the trail if it is too packed.

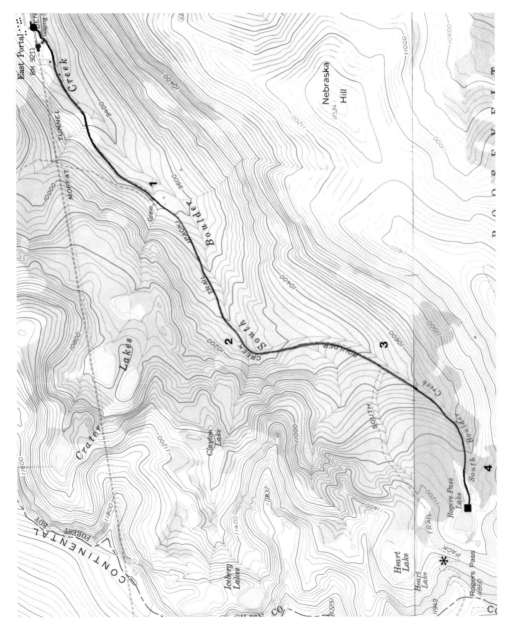

65

27 ROGERS PASS

Grade: Difficult
Distance: 11 Miles—One Way Trip
Elevation Change: 2,650 Feet
High Point: 11,860 Feet
Approximate Time: One Day
USGS Topographic Map:
   East Portal
   Empire
   Fraser

This is the shortest and fastest of the trips across the divide. It is usually done in a single day though the presence of the Pfiffner hut often prompts parties into doing this as an overnight tour. As with the other tours starting at the East Portal the restrictions on access have limited the use of this tour for the last few years. See the description for tour #24 for more details on this matter.

The tour is described as going from east to west as this is the more commonly used direction. As it starts at the East Portal and finishes near the Winter Park Ski Area, on the western side of the range, provisions for return transport must be planned. The steep slope up to Rogers Pass poses a potential avalanch hazard as do several of the gullies on the western side of the divide. While these gullies can usually be quite easily avoided the slope up to the pass must be dealt with and should not be attempted if a threat exists.

The approach and first part of this trip are described in tour #26—Rogers Pass Lake. As this description starts from the lake one should use that description to reach this point.

From the rise slightly northwest of Rogers Pass Lake the most direct route heads due west up the line of the summer trail. This involves climbing a long and very steep hillside. Most of the time this will be windblown and have very little snow. With much snow, especially if it has fallen recently, this slope can be dangerous and it is best not to proceed. Once at the top of this section gradual open slopes lead to the pass which is situated on the Continental Divide. This point is less than 5 miles from the start of the tour but the climb to here is very steep and continuous and seems much longer. From the pass the rest of the trip is visible and on a good day one can view the terrain and pick out the best way down from here.

From the pass go northwest across open tundra overlooking the Jim Creek drainage. Traverse about ¾ of a mile, passing above a very steep hillside which slopes down to the left (southwest). Then turn to the west and pick your way down the big hillside into the Jim Creek valley. At the bottom of the valley keep going to the west and cross to the south side of Jim Creek. A good trail runs along the south side of the creek and once this is located the remainder of the trip is straightforward. A long and gradual descent to the west goes quickly and this trail is often packed by skiers coming up it. The trail leads out to highway 40 at the entrance to the Mary Jane and Winter Park Ski Area.

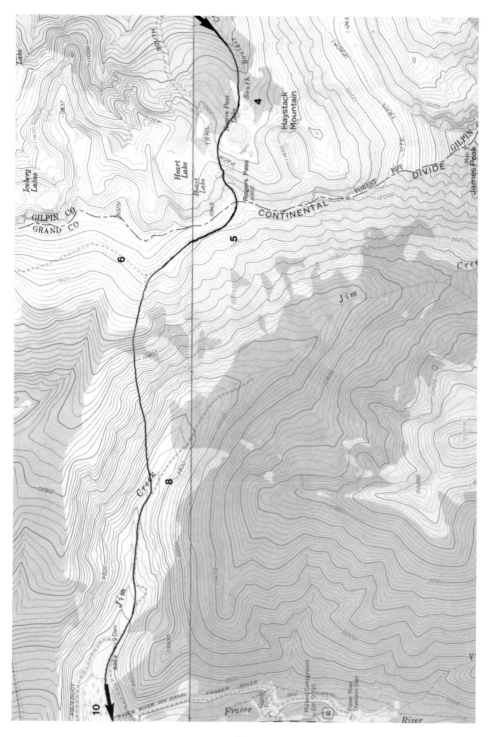

28 JAMES PEAK

Grade: Difficult
Distance: 4 Miles—One Way
Elevation Change: 2,900 Feet
High Point: 13,294 Feet
Approximate Time: One Day
USGS Topographic Map:
  Empire

At 13,294' James Peak is the most prominent summit in the southern part of the Front Range. Its high rocky summit provides outstanding views of the surrounding area and the other peaks in the range. The St. Marys Glacier is popular as an off season ski area with both downhill and cross country skiers. It is a permanent snow and ice formation and can be skied very early and very late in the season.

The open tundra and rocky slopes on the way up to the peak are often windy and blown bare, so some walking may be expected. With good snow cover this tour provides a good ski mountaineering trip and a good opportunity to do a winter ascent of a major peak. The very high elevation and the exposed nature of the tour should always be taken into account when undertaking this ascent.

Approach the start of the tour by turning off of Interstate 70 at exit 238, 2¼ miles west of Idaho Springs. This is marked as the Fall River-St. Marys Glacier exit. Drive up Fall River

Road for 8 miles, gaining a great deal of elevation. The road terminates at the St. Marys Lodge. Stop ¼ of a mile before the lodge. This is just before the road starts down to the lodge parking area and at this point a jeep road/trail goes off to the left (north). Park here, being sure not to block the road.

Cross the road and ski north along the rocky jeep trail for a few hundred yards. The road deteriorates to a trail and after ¼ mile one comes to St. Marys Lake. Go around the right (east) side of the lake to reach the foot of the St. Marys Glacier. Head west climbing along the right (north) edge of the glacier. One should take care at this point not to stray too far to the left. The further south one goes along the base of the glacier the steeper it becomes and this steep and rather avalanch prone area should be avoided. As one proceeds west along the glacier's low angled northern edge it gradually climbs and then levels off and enters a rather narrow low valley. Continue up this to the low angled and open bowl at the head of the glacier.

Climb out of this to reach a broad plateau of alpine tundra 1½ miles from the start of the tour. James Peak is obvious to the west across the plateau and appears to be much closer than it is. Head west across the tundra to reach the steeper slopes beyond. Off to the right (north) one can look across the impressive northeast face of James Peak. Climb the slopes above which are rocky with large snowpatches intermixed with boulders. The slope narrows about ½ way up, with the northeast face dropping off to the right.

Eventually the angle eases and one comes to the flat summit plateau a short distance east of the actual top. The return follows the route of ascent and is straightforward. When nearing the lower end of the glacier be sure to stay to the left to avoid the steep area.

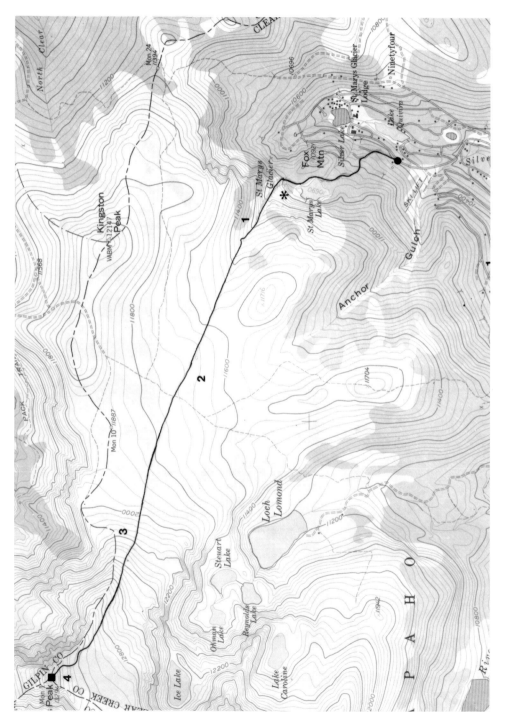

29 GUANELLA PASS

Grade: Moderate
Distance: 7½ Miles—One Way Trip
Elevation Change: 2,050 Foot Loss
High Point: 11,675 Feet
Approximate Time: Three-fourths Day
USGS Topographic Map:
  Mt. Evans

Keeping the road over Guanella Pass during the winter not only provides a convenient connection between I-70 at Georgetown and Rt. 285, but it also allows easy access to this high mountain area. This tour starts at the pass and descends the drainage of Scott Gomer Creek as it traverses below the west side of Mt. Bierstadt and then heads down to the south and southwest to intersect the Guanella Pass road at the southeast end of Geneva Park. Since most of the trip is downhill the tour goes quite rapidly. As one ends up quite a distance from the start of the trip one should be sure to plan in advance for return transportation.

Start the tour right at Guanella Pass. This can be reached either of two ways. From the north, leave I-70 at Georgetown and take the

Guanella Pass road south for 8 miles as it winds up steeply to the pass. From the south, turn off Rt. 285 at Grant and drive north on the Guanella Pass road for 14 miles, through Geneva Park to reach the top of the pass.

From the pass head southeast for about 1 mile, contouring around a knob which is off to the south. One descends slightly from this point into the open drainage of Scott Gomer Creek. Mt. Bierstadt is directly southeast from this point. Head south, down the creek valley as it passes below the western slopes of Mt. Bierstadt. After another 1½ miles the creekbed drops over a series of steep ledges. It is necessary to bypass this section by leaving the creek drainage for a short while. This is executed by heading to the east toward a low saddle between the slopes of Mt. Bierstadt and a small hill to the south of it. Once past this saddle turn south again and descend back down into the Scott Gomer creek valley near a stream fork that comes in from the east.

Ski southwest down the creek valley which is steep and a bit rocky in spots and leads on into the trees. The remainder of the trip follows the Scott Gomer Creek drainage on out to Geneva Park. After a short while one picks up a jeep trail along the stream and skis down this. It crosses the stream several times and goes in and out of the trees. Eventually one ends up on the west side of the creek. While the trail does descend steadily, there are a few short uphill sections along the way. After 7½ miles the tour ends as the trail intersects the Guanella Pass road near the southeast end of Geneva Park.

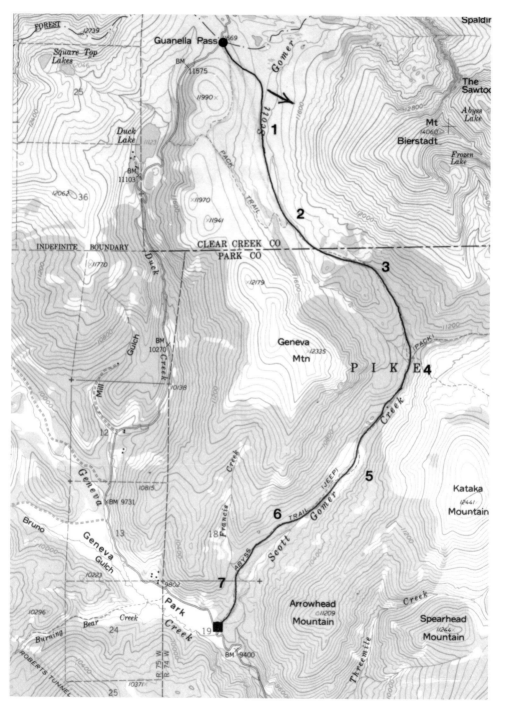

30 BUTLER GULCH

Grade: Easy-Moderate
Distance: 3 Miles—One Way
Elevation Change: 1,460 Feet
High Point: 11,450 Feet
Approximate Time: One-half Day
USGS Topographic Map:
  Empire
  Byers Peak

Of all of the tours described in this book, Butler Gulch is perhaps the one closest and most readily accessible to the Denver metropolitan area. It usually has plenty of snow and features good skiing in a pleasant setting. As a result, on weekends one often encounters large crowds of all classes of skiers as well as a goodly number of snowmobilers. Nevertheless, in its less crowded moments this trip does provide a fun tour without a long drive into the mountains.

The access road and parking are maintained by the Henderson Mine and the first part of the tour crosses that property. Skiers are asked to respect the regulations of the mine and not to cause conflicts by trespassing onto areas that are posted.

Drive west of Empire on Rt. 40 for 7½ miles to the first big hairpin turn at the base of the south side of Berthoud Pass. At this point a good road turns off to the west to the Henderson Mine. It is marked as Road 202. Drive west

on this road and after ¼ of a mile one passes a turnoff to the left. Continue 1¼ miles further to the Henderson Mine. Do NOT go straight ahead into the mine grounds. Just before the mine buildings is a turnoff to the right which is marked as the Jones Pass Road. Turn onto this and drive west along it for ¼ mile more to reach a parking area. The tour starts here.

From the parking area ski west past a gate and along a good jeep road. After ¼ mile the road forks. The right-hand branch climbs steeply up a hillside and then continues on to Jones Pass. Do not take this, but instead take the left fork of the road which leads on to Butler Gulch. Descend to the south and cross a good bridge over the West Fork of Clear Creek. Beyond the bridge the trail starts climbing more steeply. The trail zigzags a bit as it climbs up a hillside and then turns south along the west side of Butler Gulch. Keep climbing steadily along the hillside as the trail crosses a side stream coming down the steep slope on the right. Shortly after this the trail crosses the main stream in the gulch at a level area and then continues along the east side of the valley.

A long steady climb for the next ¾ of a mile leads to a series of big, wide open slopes above the treeline. Head to the west at this point and up into the broad and open area at the head of Butler Gulch. The steep slopes beyond this point should be avoided if avalanch danger exists.

The descent is fast and rather frenetic. Either ski down the trail or the steep slopes on either side of the stream to connect with the trail lower down. Follow the usually packed and fast trail down the lower part of the gulch and on out to the east to the parking area.

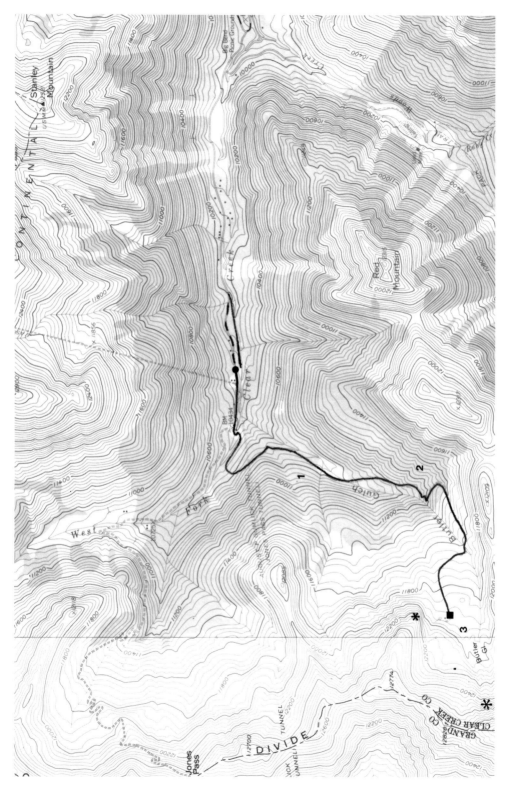

31 BERTHOUD PASS—SEVEN MILE RUN

Grade: Difficult
Distance: 3¼ Miles—One Way Trip
Elevation Change: 1,595 Foot Loss
High Point: 11,315 Feet
Approximate Time: One-fourth Day
USGS Topographic Map:
  Berthoud Pass

For many years this trail was a popular downhill ski run with Front Range skiers. When downhill areas proliferated it enjoyed a brief period of semi disuse except by a few cross-country tourers. In the last few years, with the sudden increase of emphasis on the downhill aspects of touring, the old Seven Mile Ski Trail has once again returned to popularity and is more heavily traveled than ever.

Its steep and rapid descent has a strong appeal to downhill enthusiasts and the short car shuttle or hitch back to the top of the pass often results in parties doing repeatedly in one day.

The standard trail often gets very skied out and rutted during periods of heavy use, in which case it can be quite demanding. To those who catch it after a new snowfall though it still provides a great short tour and is a good trip for working on one's downhill techniques.

Drive on Rt. 40 to the summit of Berthoud Pass. There is a large parking lot on the east side of the pass for the Berthoud Pass Ski Area and the lodge is located here also. The Seven Mile Run descends the north side of Berthoud Pass and starts from the northern edge of the ski area parking lot.

From the north edge of the lot ski down a large open hillside with scattered small pines. The highway curves back and crosses under the lower end of this slope. As one descends cut to the right (east) through a band of trees to reach a steep swath cut through the woods and which runs down to the north. Descend this and come out at a narrow clearing just to the east of a big curve of the highway.

Below this point one has a choice of two routes. One of these heads straight down staying just to the right of the road. This is the old ski trail and stays higher up on the hillside than the other route. It is the more popular of the two lines with downhill skiers as it maintains a steady drop the whole way. This trail goes more or less straight on down the valley for several miles before intersecting the road just above the lowest hairpin turn on the north side of the pass.

Most cross-country skiers prefer the other route. This is followed by cutting to the right a bit as one descends below the big curve and entering the actual stream drainage. This winds on down through the forest and across several meadows coming in from the east. After 1¼ miles one comes to a very steep drop down a long and narrow stretch of the streambed. Below this things level off and one stays to the left of the stream to soon come to a big open meadow.

Cross this and continue on down, still to the left of the creek. The last mile follows a trail down through more open forest. This section gives a fast and steady descent with many winding turns and bumps to add to the excitement of things. Eventually it levels off and the trail leads out to the highway at the lowest hairpin turn on the north side of the pass.

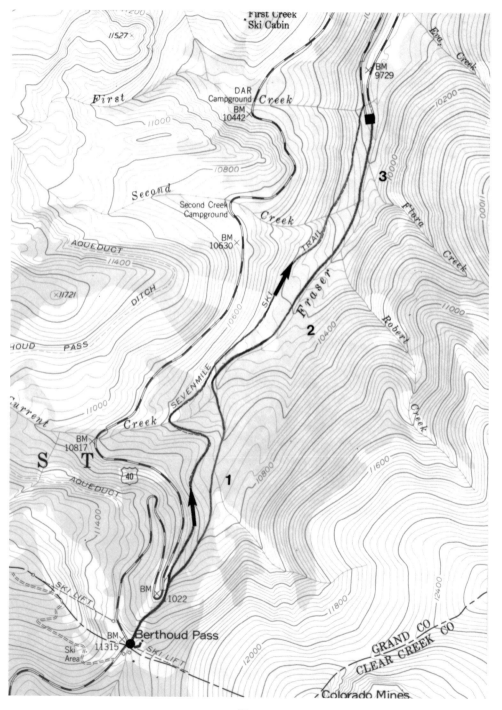

32 SECOND CREEK

Grade: Easy
Distance: 1¼ Miles—One Way
Elevation Change: 750 Feet
High Point: 11,350 Feet
Approximate Time: One-fourth Day
USGS Topographic Map:
  Berthoud Pass

The short tour up to the A-frame cabin on the ridge between Second Creek and First Creek is a fun and easy ski. Due to the high elevation of the valley and its location a lot of snow accumulates and it has a longer season than some of the other tours described in this book. The ascent is fairly steady, though gradual, and approximately the first half of the tour is wooded while the second part is out in the open. The moderate angle of the slopes in the upper section are a good place for beginners to practice some downhill skiing.

A considerable avalanch danger can sometimes exist along the south and southwest sides of the valley. This can be easily avoided simply by staying well away from these areas. When using the hut please be sure to keep it clean and abide by any posted regulations. Sometimes parties like to do this tour as a followup to the Seven Mile Tour—#31—to get in a full day of skiing in the Berthoud Pass area without repeating that trip.

To reach the start of the tour drive on Rt. 40 down the north side of Berthoud Pass. Second Creek is the middle, or second, of the 3 major drainages that run up on the west side of the road. Stop at the large curve just over 3 miles north of the summit of the pass. There is usually parking along the road at this turn as well as just downhill from it. Start skiing on the west side of the road at the outside of the large curve. Head up the wide and gradual valley to the west. It is best to stay on the right (north) side of the creek. The skiing is through open forests which become even more scattered as one climbs. Care should be taken to stay well clear of the steep slopes on the south side of the valley. Soon one will emerge from the trees and continue on to the west gradually gaining elevation up the open hillsides. Then head in a northwesterly direction and ski up toward a low saddle on the ridge that runs along the north side of the Second Creek valley. Be sure to do this well before the large and very steep area at the western end of the Second Creek drainage.

Near the top of the ridge turn west again and ski easily up to the small A-frame cabin which is tucked in by a clump of trees near the crest of the ridge. From the cabin it is quite straightforward to continue on up to the northwest into the upper end of the First Creek valley. By continuing up to the west on low-angled and open terrain to the west of this one can reach the top of the main north-south ridge after 1¼ more miles. The descent from the cabin is quick and fun. Simply ski down the way one came up and reach the road in a short time.

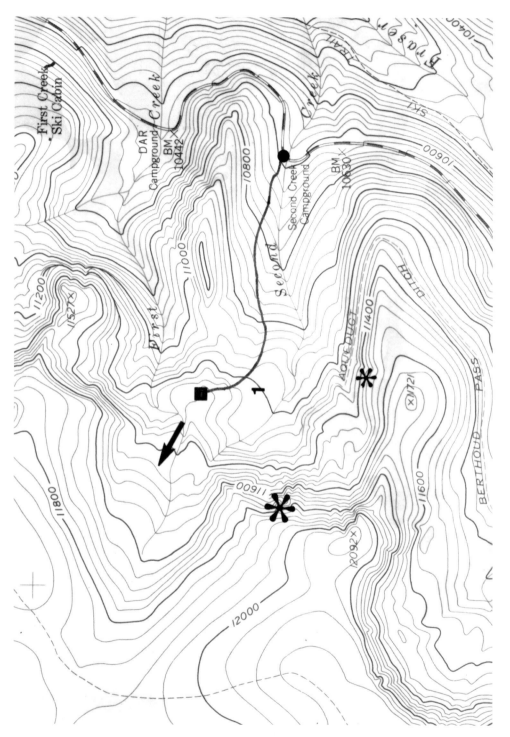

33 JIM CREEK

Grade: Easy
Distance: 3½ Miles—One Way
Elevation Change: 820 Feet
High Point: 10,050 Feet
Approximate Time: One-half Day
USGS Topographic Map:
  Fraser
  Empire
  East Portal

Jim Creek is located directly across the road from the Mary Jane Ski Area. The traffic from downhill skiers going to that area often gives the trailhead a rather frenzied atmosphere. Once one leaves the environs of the roadside however, all of that is soon left behind. Harboring lots of snow and providing striking views of the western side of the Front Range, the gradual and gliding run up the Jim Creek valley is a favored trip for many skiers.

Reach the start of the tour by driving along Rt. 40 to the entrance of the Mary Jane Ski Area. This is 10 miles north of the summit of Berthoud Pass. Park along the highway at an area that is usually plowed out.

Start skiing on the east side of the road and head east along the south side of the valley. This first part of the ski is on a snowcovered road. After ¼ of a mile one passes under a large aquaduct pipe. Keep heading east as the trail gradually climbs and the skiing is near the edge of the trees. The trail goes in and out of the forest as it runs up along the south side of a series of clearings. After 1½ miles traverse a large meadow with many old tree stumps. Beyond this the trail steepens and the terrain becomes more forested. Continue on to the east on the trail, which is still on the south side of the valley, and eventually it narrows and steepens even more as the drainage narrows. Many skiers choose to stop here and head back down. One can proceed on beyond this staying near the streambed as the climb soon levels off. Easy skiing along the left side of the creek crosses a series of clearings in the forest. Eventually the tour steepens again, still following the stream. Those who continue on beyond this point will come to a series of high open bowls below the steep headwalls at the upper end of the valley. Most skiers seem to choose to stop before the treeline and head on back.

The return trip retraces one's tracks down the valley all the way to the road. The long and steady descent is a quick and rather exhilerating run. The lower section is normally packed and lower angled.

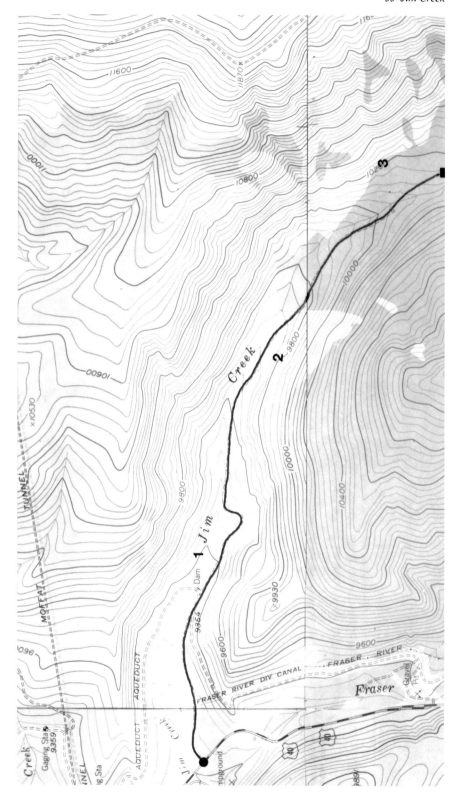

34 RABBIT EARS PEAK

Grade: Moderate
Distance: 4½ Miles—One Way
Elevation Change: 1,080 Feet
High Point: 10,654 Feet
Approximate Time: One Day
USGS Topographic Map:
 Rabbit Ears Peak

Few, if any, areas of Colorado can rival Rabbit Ears Pass for the quality and quantity of its snow. It is an excellent area for early or late season skiing and its high, rolling terrain is ideally suited for ski touring. Unfortunately it is a long way from the main population centers of the state but those who go there will find the quality of the skiing will more than make up for the travel involved in getting there.

It is important to note that the topographic map of this area is seriously outdated and does not show the current road over the pass. This feature has been drawn in on the map in this book that accompanies this description. Rabbit Ears Peak is prominent from the road as one nears the pass and the tour for the most part either follows the main divide more or less, or goes along an old jeep road which is never far from the ridgeline of the divide.

The trip starts from highway 40 at the east summit of Rabbit Ears Pass, approximately 20 miles east of the town of Steamboat Springs. There is parking at a plowed turnoff area and a large "Continental Divide" sign marks the start of the trip.

From the north side of the road ski north and slightly west for ½ mile. This takes one across meadows along the west side of the actual crest of the divide ridge. At the north end of the meadows one reenters the woods and picks up an old roadbed. Continue along this taking the left fork when the road divides. This part of the tour is often used by snowmobiles and at the 1¼ milepoint one crosses the remains of the old Rt. 40 near a large stone edifice in a clearing. At this point of the tour Rabbit Ears Peak is visible to the north. Continue north along the divide and then follow an old trail just to the east of the actual ridge crest. After ¼ of a mile this road splits and one should take the right (eastern) fork. This veers a bit to the east and then heads north again, traversing a series of meadows as it heads up a shallow streambed and an open valley. These will gradually merge into the main hillside west of Grizzly Creek and the road stays on this hillside on the left of the creek as it continues further north.

After 3¼ miles from the start of the trip the road makes a big loop back around to the right and turns to the south east as it starts climbing up the southwest facing slopes of Rabbit Ears Peak. One can either short-cut straight up the hillside and bypass this loop, or keep following the road which is a longer but more gradual alternative. Soon the road curves left, and goes north a little to the short final climb leading to the summit of Rabbit Ears Peak.

The return trip reverses the tour in. The steady descent down the tracks is pleasant and offers long gliding runs down the gradual, but steady grade.

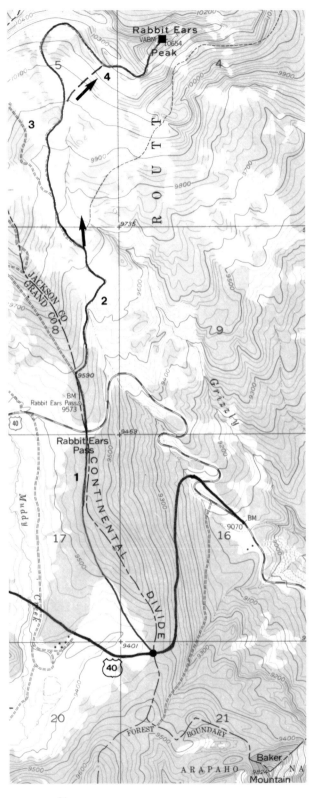

35 LOVELAND PASS

Grade: Moderate
Distance: 1 or 2½ Miles—One Way Trip
Elevation Change: North Side—1,310 Foot Loss
South Side—990 Foot Loss
High Point: 11,990 Feet
Approximate Time: One-fourth Day—Each Tour
USGS Topographic Map:
Loveland Pass
Grays Peak

At almost 12,000' Loveland Pass is one of the highest year-round passes in the state. It is located in the heart of the state's ski country and the view from the summit is one of truly spectacular alpine scenery. Due to the very high elevation the road conditions can be very bad and one should check on these if they are at all questionable when planning the trip. This tour actually consists of two very steep and rather short downill runs. Both of these are popular with downhill skiers as well as tourers, especially the one on the north side of the pass. On a good weekend the scene may more closely resemble one of the nearby downhill areas than an area of high mountain touring. As the longer tour on the south side of the pass has a fairly flat stretch at the bottom it is more frequently done by cross-country skiers and is the less popular of the two.

The skiing starts well above the treeline and high winds and windpacked crust are not uncommon on the upper part of the trips. Skiers should be prepared for adverse weather, especially cold temperatures and wind. Both of these tours terminate at the roadside near the base of the pass close to downhill ski areas. As the prospect of a return climb is distinctly uninviting many parties set up a car shuttle in advance. Usually hitching a ride back to the top of the pass is quick and simple and many skiers resort to this means of return transportation.

The approach is by following Rt. 6 either from I-70, to the north, or from the vicinity of Keystone and A-Basin, to the south. Either way, follow the road all the way to the summit of Loveland Pass and park in a turnoff on the east side of the road.

NORTH SIDE—Start by skiing west from the summit of the pass. A faint trail contours down to the west along a rocky and wind swept hillside as it leads down into broad and open bowls. Once at this point turn north and ski downhill in a broad and steep drainage system towards the trees below. After a fast and steep ½ mile descent one arrives at the road. One can stop here and return to the top of the pass or continue across the road and down more gentle terrain to the Loveland Valley Ski Area. The latter choice starts down steeply at first but soon moderates. The best route is to follow the stream drainage and after another mile one reaches the upper end of the ski area. Ski down the prepared runs to their base and connect with the road.

SOUTH SIDE—From the parking area on the east side of Loveland Pass swing out to the east and southeast and descend for ½ mile into a big, wide open valley. Curve off to the east to stay above a large curve of the road and then head down to the south. Stay to the left (east) of the road as one descends into the less steep section below. Another mile of skiing which levels out as one goes further ends at the road near the base of the pass. One can extend this tour slightly by skirting around the east end of a big curve and then skiing for another ¼ mile to arrive at the A-Basin Ski Area.

82

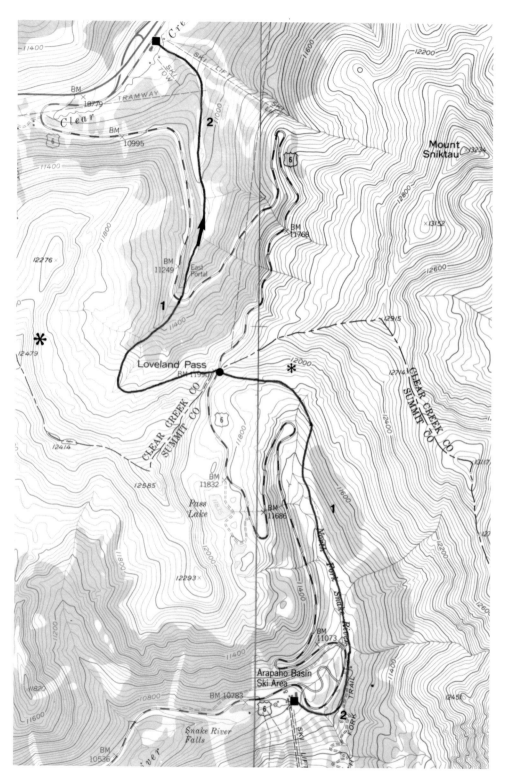

36 PERU CREEK

Grade: Easy-Moderate
Distance: 4½ Miles—One Way
Elevation Change: 920 Feet
High Point: 10,950 Feet
Approximate Time: One Day
USGS Topographic Map:
Montezuma

Peru Creek is one of the many side drainages of the Snake River, west of the Keystone Ski Area. Most of these subsidiary valleys have old mining roads and the remains of old mines in them and are frequently used in winter by cross-country skiers. The valley of Peru Creek harbors a number of mine sites and in the summer a dirt road leads up the valley to these. This wide and gradually angled drainage offers an easy and pleasant tour. Most skiers will make the old buildings of the Pennsylvania Mine site their goal. A backdrop of high mountain scenery behind these weathered remnants of the mine forms a quaint and scenic, and much photographed stop. Stronger tourers seeking a longer trip can continue on up to Horseshoe Basin at the head of the valley or turn off to the north part way along this tour and go north to explore the upper reaches of Chihuahua and Ruby Gulches.

The start of this tour is reached by turning south off of Rt. 6 about 1¼ miles east of the Keystone Ski Area onto the Montezuma Road. Almost immediately this road divides. Do not take the right-hand fork which leads to the ski area, but stay with the main road as it heads to the east along the Snake River. After 4½ miles (and 1 mile before the town of Montezuma) one crosses the river on a good bridge as the road bends sharply left and then almost immediately it curves back to the right. At this point the Peru Creek road turns off to the left, on the north side of the main road. Park here along the road, being careful not to block through traffic.

Start skiing on the side road which leads north through the forest for ¼ mile before turning to the east into the main valley of Peru Creek. Ski for 1 mile along the south side of the creek. The trail seems almost level but does gradually climb and traverses some open meadows and then crosses to the north side of the creek. For 1 mile more one skis east up the valley, passes the old Maid of Orleans Mine, and comes to some wide clearings at the mount of Chihuahua Gulch which comes in from the left (north).

The next 1¼ miles cross meadows and go through some wooded sections as the trail keeps going east along the north side of Peru Creek. Then, at a fork in the road, take the right-hand fork and cross back to the south side of the creek. Continue on to the east up a slight grade to reach the many old buildings of the Pennsylvania Mine site.

The return trip heads west, back down the valley following one's tracks to reach the road.

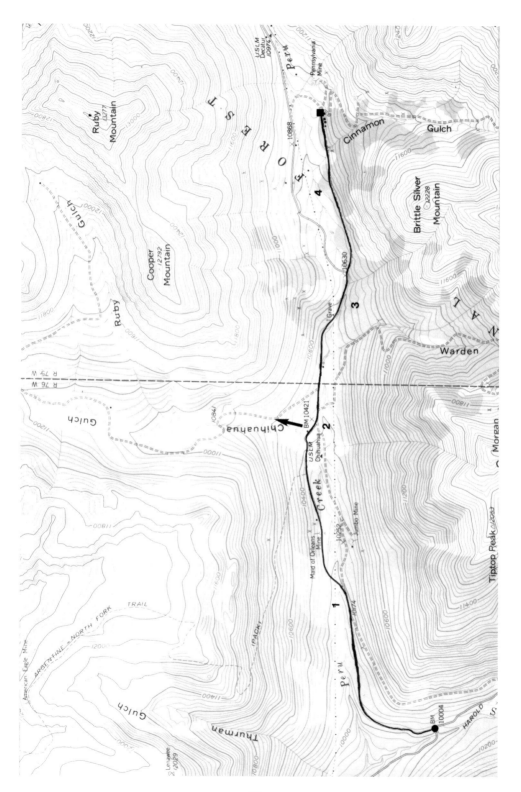

37 STS. JOHN GULCH

Grade: Moderate
Distance: 3½ Miles—One Way
Elevation Change: 1,400 Feet
High Point: 11,680 Feet
Approximate Time: One Day
USGS Topographic Map:
  Keystone
  Montezuma

Saints John Gulch is the shortest and steepest of the tours described near Montezuma. It starts right at the old town and follows an old mining road, passing through the old town site of Sts. John and the mine ruins and then winds on up to the site of the Wild Irishman Mine. This tour is used frequently by parties engaged in longer tours to connect with either the Keystone Ski Area by traversing the ridgeline, or by parties crossing the main ridge and continuing on to the Tiger or Breckenridge areas. The broad open slopes at the upper end of the valley are areas of avalanch potential and should be avoided when this danger exists.

At a point 1¼ miles east of the Keystone Ski Area turn south off of Rt. 6 onto the Montezuma Road. This divides almost immediately. Do not take the right-hand fork back to the ski area, but drive along the main road (left fork) as it heads east along the Snake River. After

almost six miles one reaches a cluster of buildings which constitute the town of Montezuma. Park at the south end of the town in a turnout on the right side of the road.

Ski along an old mining road which descends to the west and soon crosses a bridge over the Snake River. On the Southwest side of the river the road turns sharply to the right and climbs to the northwest through the forest past the road turning off to the old Equity Mine site. After ¼ of a mile the road zigzags up the hillside and then turns left (southwest) to reach a trail junction in a meadow at the mouth of the Sts. John Creek valley. Now ski to the southwest along the east edge of the meadow and then back into the woods. The trail climbs more steeply as one proceeds along the left side of the creek for the next ½ mile. Then the road crosses to the right (west) side of the creek and before much longer one passes some old buildings. These mark the townsite of Sts. John and the mine site is up to the east.

Very soon the road climbs steeply up on the hillside to the right and along this, crossing some steep open slopes. Most skiers prefer at this point to directly follow the streambed up the valley and rejoin the road ½ mile further on. Continue skiing to the southwest, up the drainage as the touring alternates between forests and open meadows. At the 2½ mile point the road starts curving to the left, heading toward the southeast up a much steeper incline. After another ¾ of a mile of climbing the trail curves sharply to the left (north) near the treeline and leads to the Wild Irishman Mine.

The descent reverses the tour in, down the road and drainage. It descends steadily and the return trip goes quite rapidly.

86

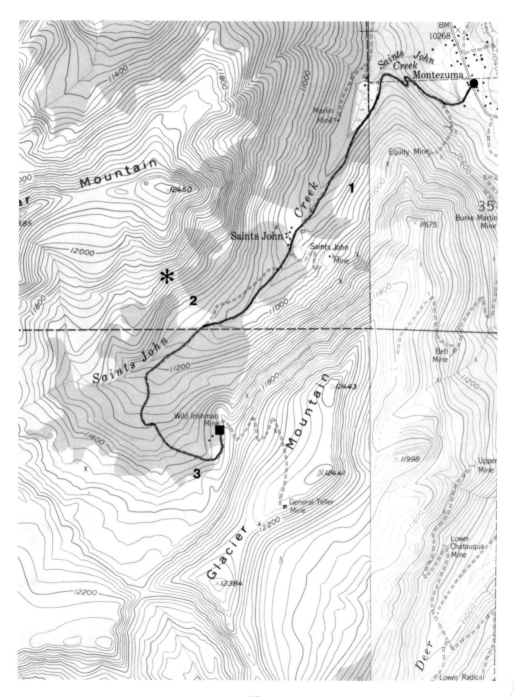

38 DEER CREEK

Grade: Easy
Distance: 3 Miles—One Way
Elevation Change: 850 Feet
High Point: 11,280 Feet
Approximate Time: One-half Day
USGS Topographic Map:
 Montezuma

The Deer Creek valley is a good tour in the Montezuma region for beginning skiers who want to go off and see a bit of the back country. The elevation gain is minimal and the skiing is quite easy. Since most of the tour follows an old road along the valley bottom there is virtually no route finding. Though the trip is below the treeline and on the valley bottom much of the skiing is across large clearings and one has good views and large amounts of the route are usually visible. The steep slopes to the southwest at the head of the valley may occasionally pose an avalanch threat, however these should be avoided and the course stays well away from them.

At a point 1¼ miles east of the Keystone Ski Area turn south off of Rt. 6 onto the Montezuma Road. This divides almost immediately. Do not take the right-hand fork which goes back to the ski area but stay on the main road (the left fork) as it heads east along the Snake River. Drive east almost 6 miles to pass through the town of Montezuma. Continue straight ahead for ½ mile more to the end of the plowed road where there are usually several plowed parking areas.

From the end of the plowed road ski directly south along the unplowed road. After about 200 yards the Webster Pass road turns off to the left (east) and one continues straight ahead toward the Deer Creek valley.

After about ⅓ of a mile the old mining road that one is following crosses to the right (west) side of the creek. At this point a road turns off to the right (northwest) to the Superior Mine. Ski on south heading up the valley for another ½ mile passing an old building on the right of the road and come to a long clearing. The tour continues along the road which runs parallel to the creek and stays near the right (west) side of this clearing and wanders in and out of the woods. One soon crosses a stream that comes down from the west.

Very gradually gain elevation along the valley floor and two miles from the start of the tour one comes to a T-junction of the mining roads. These lead up to old mines to the northwest and southeast. The simplest thing to do here is to continue straight ahead up the drainage and forsake the road, skiing along the creek instead. Continue on this course to the end of the clearings and then climb somewhat more steeply, still following the creek, through a short wooded section. Beyond this the valley floor levels off again and one arrives at another long clearing. In the summer there are several shallow ponds here and this point is usually the end of the tour. As the valley walls get much steeper beyond this point it is advisable to turn around and start the return trip which retraces one's tracks back out to the parking area.

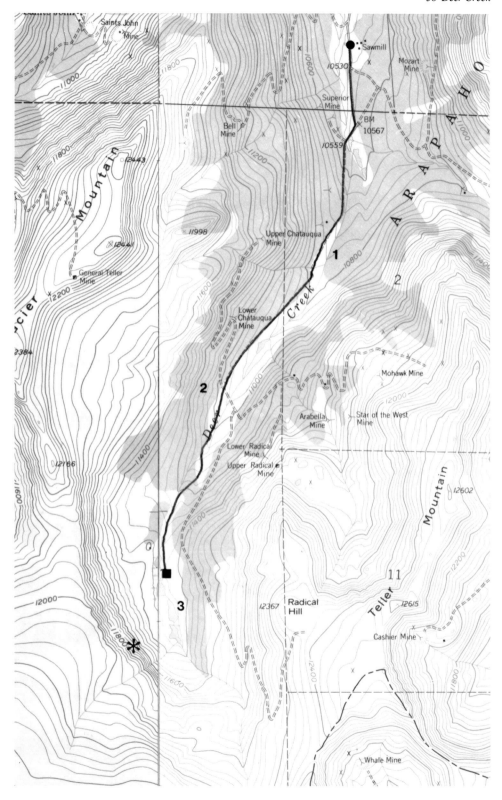

39 SNAKE RIVER VALLEY TO WEBSTER PASS

Grade: Easy-Moderate
Distance: 3½ Miles—One Way
Elevation Change: 870 Feet
High Point: 11,400 Feet
Approximate Time: One-half Day
USGS Topographic Map:
Montezuma

This tour starts just beyond Montezuma and travels up the valley of the Snake River to its upper terminus. Most parties usually turn around at the upper end of the valley but those who press on all the way to Webster Pass will find the views of the surrounding peaks and South Park to be well worth the effort. The skiing is not very difficult as most of the tour is very gradual, but the last section up to the pass itself is considerably steeper. The upper half of the valley is open and often can be quite windy. Snowmobiles use this drainage a fair amount and especially on weekends one cannot help but notice their presence, although their paths often make the skiing considerably easier.

At a point 1¼ miles east of the Keystone Ski Area turn south off of Rt. 6 onto the Montezuma Road. This divides almost immediately and one should not take the right-hand fork which returns to the ski area, but should stay with the main branch of the road as it heads east along the Snake River. Drive east for almost 6 miles and pass through the old town of Montezuma. Continue straight ahead for ½ mile more to the end of the plowed road. There are usually several plowed parking areas here.

Ski directly south along the unplowed road for about 200 yards. At this point turn left (east) onto the old mining road that heads up the Snake River drainage toward Webster Pass. The trail winds up through the woods, climbing

an easy hill for ½ mile and then passes a large open slope which is just up to the left of the trail. This area provides an excellent spot to practice some downhill techniques. The tour continues to the southeast climbing slightly as it goes along the left side of the stream and soon passes a side road that runs off to the north. Further on one passes an old building and leaves the forest behind. Ski along the open valley staying on the left side of the stream for another ¾ of a mile and then cross to the right side of it. Proceed below an open hillside with many tree stumps and eventually the road nears the margin of the trees along the west side of the clearings.

On calm days many skiers prefer to more directly follow the stream course, but if it is windy a route closer to the trees is more sheltered. For another mile the valley stays fairly level as one skis easily along, gradually gaining a slight bit of elevation and crossing an area of beaver activity. After another ¼ mile the valley floor steepens and one must climb a short rise to reach the broad and open section beyond. The summer mining road, which is usually obscured by snow, forks at this point. The right-hand branch goes up to the west to the Cashier Mine high on the side of Teller Mountain, while the left fork goes on up to Webster Pass. Many parties choose to stop here, after 3½ miles of skiing and take a break by the last trees which are just off to the left before heading down. If it is not too windy or if one is not too tired, Webster Pass is only about ¾ of a mile to the southeast. The road zigzags up the open and rocky hillside which is often wind-blown and is obvious from below.

The return trip follows one's tracks back down the valley in a long and gently gliding descent.

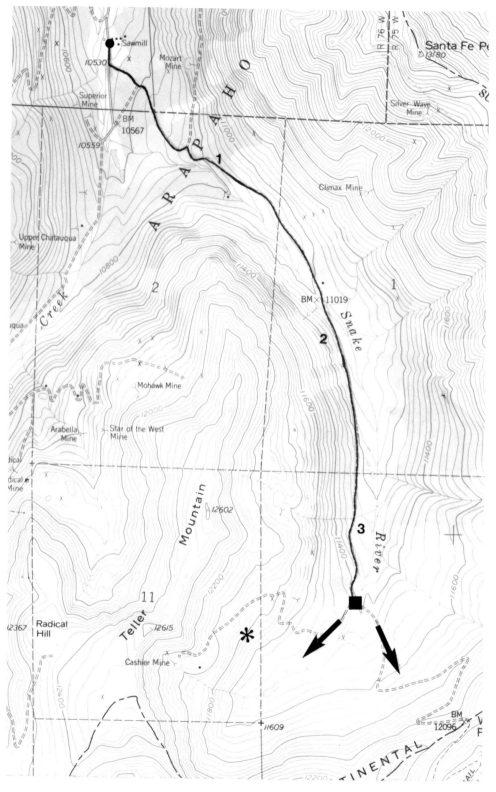

40 BRECKENRIDGE TO FRISCO

Grade: Easy
Distance: 8½ Miles—One Way Trip
Elevation Change: 830 Foot Loss
High Point: 10,250 Feet
Approximate Time: One-half to One Day
USGS Topographic Map:
  Breckenridge
  Frisco

Although this tour can be done in either direction it is described here as going from south to north, or from Breckenridge to Frisco. That way the net change in elevation for the rolling course is a loss of just over 800′ rather than a gain. The entire tour lies below treeline and is quite sheltered. Usually at least the northern half of the course is tracked by local skiers and except after a recent snowfall the entire trip usually has packed tracks. As the tour ends a considerable distance from the starting point one should either arrange a car shuttle or plan to hitch back. It may be possible to catch a shuttle bus from Frisco to the Breckenridge Ski Area but this varies from year to year and one is advised to check locally on this.

Drive to the south end of the town of Breckenridge. At a traffic light turn west on Ski Hill Road which is plainly marked. Drive up Ski Hill Road past a touring center and continue west past the downhill ski area. Just above the downhill ski area is a sharp U-turn. Park here in a large area.

Start skiing north from the northwest corner of the parking area at the U-turn. The trail is usually well marked with red flagging tape. The trail heads north closely following the 10,000′ contour line on the Breckenridge topo map.

The terrain is fairly level and rolling though there is a slight bit of elevation gain before crossing Cucumber Creek. Beyond the creek one continues north contouring the hillside and then descending a little and crossing a clearing. Soon one connects with an old road and skis north along this for a couple of hundred yards to a junction. Up to this point the route is normally marked with flags.

At the junction head up the left fork and almost immediately turn off onto a good trail. From here north all the way to Frisco the tour is usually tracked by the local high school nordic team. Continue north as the trail still roughly follows the 10,000′ contour line on the map and as it goes out over the low ridge north of South Barton Gulch the route veers to the right and drops a couple of hundred feet, crossing Middle Barton Gulch and then goes out into North Barton Gulch. At this point one breaks out of the woods into some open meadows below some small ponds.

The ski trail heads northwest along a creekbed, staying on the left side of the creek and climbs gradually for about a mile to reach a low pass. This is marked "X 10,022" on the Breckenridge topographic quadrangle. Beyond this low saddle one drops down to the north into the Miners Creek valley and soon picks up an old road on the east side of the creek. Like the rest of the tour the section from Barton Gulch to Miners Creek is tracked and marked with red tape flags.

Ski north following the road along the west side of Miners Creek for another couple of miles. Many trails and tracks are often encountered in this section but the best route takes this line. This section is a long and gradual descent and alternates between wooded sections and open meadows. At the north end of the valley the road turns sharply to the northeast and soon connects with a plowed road. Proceed along this for ½ mile to reach Rt. 9 near the highway maintainence garage.

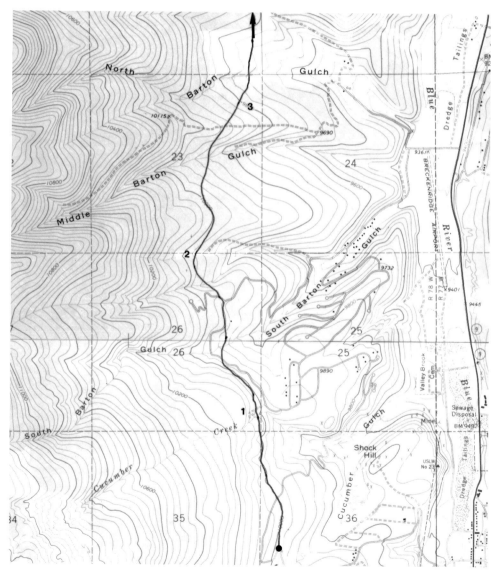

93

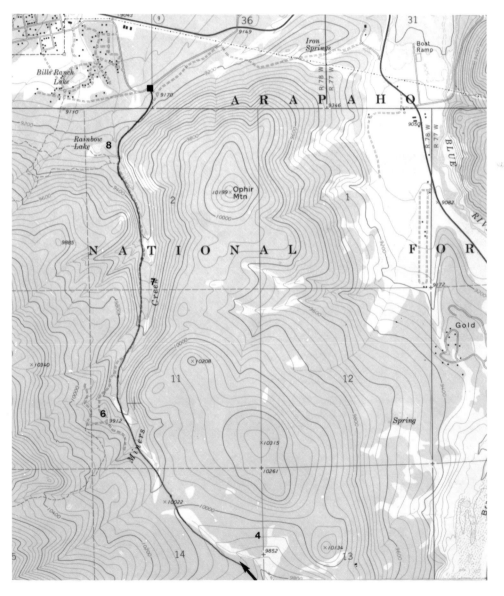

95

41 BOREAS PASS

Grade: Easy-Moderate
Distance: 8 Miles—One Way
Elevation Change: 1,140 Feet
High Point: 11,481 Feet
Approximate Time: One Day
USGS Topographic Map:
Breckenridge
Boreas Pass

Starting in Illinois Gulch this tour follows an old railroad bed and ascends gradually but continuously as it climbs well above treeline and terminates at 11,481′ Boreas Pass. The easy gradient makes it a good tour for less proficient skiers and since the trip does follow an old railroad grade the route finding is not any problem. Many parties choose to turn around at the old water tank, a scenic spot which makes a logical breaking point on the tour. The long and open climb up from there provides magnificent views of the surrounding mountains though this section is very exposed to the elements, especially the wind.

Take Rt. 9 to the south end of the town of Breckenridge, and the junction with the Boreas Pass Road. Turn off to the east on to the Boreas Pass Road and follow it for 3½ miles as it winds up Illinois Gulch. After the first mile one encounters a sharp hairpin turn to the left, then the road makes a long turn back to the right around Barney Ford Hill. About 3 miles from the turnoff from Rt. 9 one comes to an intersection and the road curves back up to the right. Park just beyond this point.

Start skiing up along the Boreas Pass Road, which is the old railroad grade. It initially heads to the southwest, passing Rocky Point as it goes through road cuts and travels in and out of the woods. After ½ mile the road curves sharply left and heads southeast, a course which it more or less follows for the rest of the tour. Climb gradually but steadily as the grade heads along the southwest facing hillside above Indiana Creek. After 1½ miles the road curves sharply left, and then back right, passing a side road that comes in from the north. As the roadbed climbs steadily it has several small curves and wiggles and passes through numerous wooded sections. At the 3½ mile point it rounds a prominent ridge and curves sharply to the left into a side stream valley. Just before turning to the right again and crossing the stream one arrives at Bakers Tank. This is an old water tank used by the trains when this route was actively used by the railroad. This is an obvious point at which to stop for a break, and/or turn around if not continuing all the way to the pass.

The skiing is much the same for the next mile, at which point another side stream comes down from the left. One more mile after this brings one to some old buildings and beyond this the tour breaks out of the trees. The next mile of skiing crosses open and low-angled hillsides and then the roadbed begins to head more to the south. Another ½ mile of steady climbing along the roadbed leads on beyond this across the slopes which are often blown clear by the wind and lead up to Boreas Pass.

The return trip reverses the tour exactly. If the snow is firm and the tracks are good the long steady descent can be done quite quickly and easily.

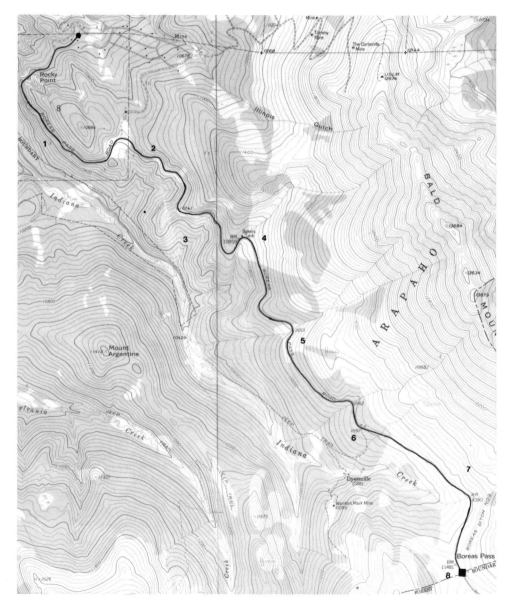

42 SOUTH WILLOW CREEK

Grade: Easy
Distance: 4½ Miles—One Way
Elevation Change: 230 Feet
High Point: 9,600 Feet
Approximate Time: One Day
USGS Topographic Map:
  Frisco
  Dillon

Sheltered and in the forest for almost its entire length the South Willow Creek tour is pleasant and fun. It has been described as perhaps the only tour that goes downhill in both directions. While this is not entirely true, the rolling nature of the trip certainly creates that impression. The old cabin at the end of the trip is in pretty reasonable condition and is frequently used by parties of skiers seeking an easy overnight outing. The start of the tour is rather odd, being located in the midst of a residential development, so one should use consideration with respect to parking and the local inhabitants.

Turn off I-70 at the Silverthorne-Dillon exit. Drive north on Rt. 9 a very short distance and cross the Blue River. Take the next left turn after crossing the river, onto a dirt road. Go south on this for ¼ of a mile and just before passing back under the Interstate turn off to the right. Almost immediately this road divides and one should take the right-hand fork which heads up to the west. Very soon this road makes a sharp turn back left and then curves back to

the right again. At a point ¾ of a mile from where one turned onto this last road one reaches a side road that comes in on the north. Turn sharply back up to the right onto this and drive along it for ½ mile. At this point turn left at a junction and go up another ¼ mile until this road makes a sharp turn to the right. Park here as the trail starts on the north side of the road and is marked by signs.

Ski north on a well marked trail, the Dillon Pack Trail. This runs along fences marking private land as one heads northwest through the forest and soon after leaving the houses behind crosses an open meadow. Beyond this the trail curves slightly to the left and at the ½ mile point one reaches a big open hillside running down to the right. Head northwest across this and reenter the woods. Then the trail curves west, crosses a small brook, and after another ½ mile zigzags as it climbs through an open forest. Steeper climbing then leads onto a low ridge and then the trail goes west along this. Soon one turns to the right and crosses a small stream drainage and then contours along the hillside heading in a northeasterly direction.

At the 2½ mile point the trail rounds the prow of the ridge and descends steeply to the northwest for a short distance to intersect the Wheeler Jeep Trail. Turn left on this and ski to the west, descending for another ½ mile into the bottom of the South Willow Creek drainage. Cross the creek and pass a trail junction with a trail coming in from the north. Keep going west along South Willow Creek and soon the trail climbs up a little and out of the actual creekbed. Ski through some flat meadows and pine woods along the bench on the north side of the creek to reach the old cabin.

This structure is located near the west end of an open meadow and marks the best spot to end the tour. Beyond this point the valley becomes very steep and narrow and in a short distance the thick forest will make progress difficult. Due to these reasons most tourers prefer to stop at the cabin and turn around. The return trip reverses the ski in exactly and takes almost the same amount of time as the trip in did.

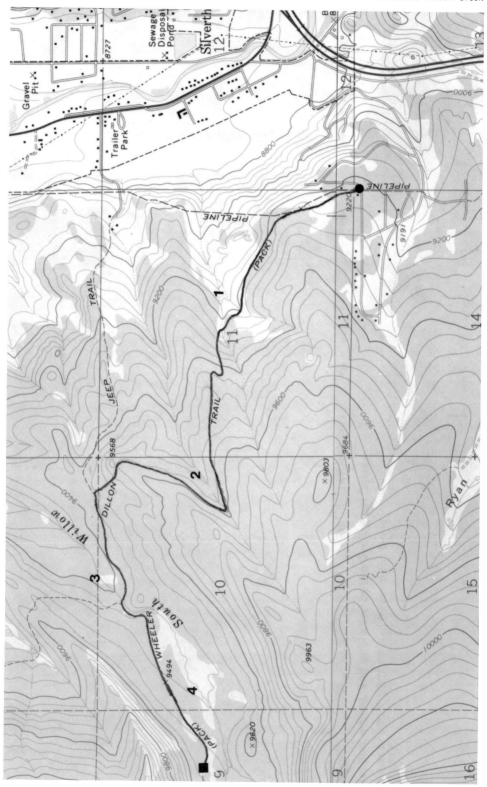

43 NORTH TEN MILE CREEK

Grade: Moderate
Distance: 6 Miles—One Way
Elevation Change: 1,250 Feet
High Point: 10,350 Feet
Approximate Time: One Day
USGS Topographic Map:
   Frisco
   Vail Pass

Few tours are more easily reached than this one. The skiing starts immediately from the western Frisco Exit off of I-70. This also makes North Ten Mile Creek popular with snowmobilers and they are frequently encountered in this valley on weekends. After the initial steep section the tour is really quite gradual as it wanders along the valley bottom. The first mile of the trip is often hardpacked and icy, especially at the steep part. When descending this short and narrow section it is often worth considering walking down the worst part if it is icy or if there is not much snow. The upper valley usually has lots of good snow and has pleasant and scenic skiing. After 3-3½ miles from the road there are a series of long open slopes on the north side of the valley. With the recent surge of interest in "Telemarking" these are becoming a very popular objective with tourers.

The start is easily reached by turning off of I-70 at the western of the two exists for Frisco. On the north side of the Interstate is a dirt road that heads off to the west. From the bottom of the exit ramp park on the north side of the Interstate being sure not to block the road.

Ski west from the parking area up the dirt road, which angles to the left slightly and soon leads past some water tanks. This road is often plowed to this point. After about ½ mile the road forks and one normally takes the right-hand fork, though the two variations soon rejoin. For the next ½ mile the trail climbs very steeply up a wooded hillside and is quite narrow in spots. At the top of the steep section the trail levels off and soon goes past a small pond. For the next ½ mile one continues along the north side of the stream through woods and past the old sight of the Prospect Mine. The trail then leads through some meadows and past another small pond before reaching a clearing that runs down from the north. The next mile stays in the woods on the hillside above the stream and is marked occasionally. Then one skis down a short drop and crosses to the south side of the stream and then proceeds along this for another ½ mile before crossing back into the woods on the north side of the creek.

This section of the trail is not well marked and frequently a large number of snowmobile tracks can add to ones problems in picking out the route. However, the tour basically just parallels North Ten Mile Creek as it heads west near the floor of the valley. A little over 3 miles from the start of the tour one comes to a large open slope that extends a long way up the hillside to the right (north). This is the first of several of such clearings. Cross to the far side of the open area and continue west, staying slightly uphill from the creek and on its north side. Beyond the area of these open slopes the trail is better marked and more easily followed. It leads on through pine forests and at the 4½ mile point a trail junction is reached which is marked by signs.

Keep heading west as the skiing is more level and soon come to a long open meadow. Up to the right of this are more open slopes dotted with tree stumps. From here on the valley is quite flat and open, affording fine views. Further along the valley curves to the northwest slightly and at this point, if not sooner, most parties chose to head back. Those who do continue will find that the valley eventually terminates in a series of steep slopes. The return trip follows ones tracks back out to the east.

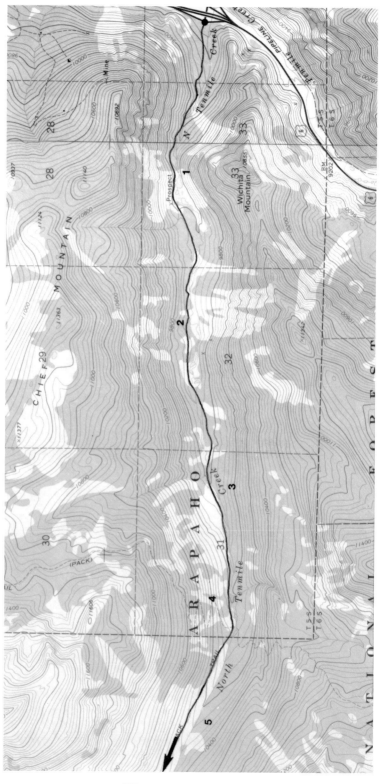

44 MAYFLOWER GULCH

Grade: Moderate
Distance: 3 Miles—One Way
Elevation Change: 1,025 Feet
High Point: 11,560 Feet
Approximate Time: One Day
USGS Topographic Map:
  Copper Mountain

The Mayflower Gulch tour is another "favorite". Though it is not very long, the steady climb going in and the coresponding descent on the return combine with the fairly high elevation of the trip to make it more of an outing than the distance implies. Also, there are two additional attractions to this tour. The first of these is the old Boston Mine sight. This has several old buildings, some of which have been fixed up and are maintained in a fairly habitable state. Consequently one has a comfortable shelter to stop in at the upper end of the tour when the weather is bad. Also, these are often used by skiers wishing to spend the night in the gulch. Please be sure however, to keep the cabins clean and to abide by any requirements as to their use and maintainance. The second feature of Mayflower Gulch is the large scenic basin at the upper end of the valley. The bowls

here can furnish exceptional powder skiing when the conditions are right. On a sunny day with good snow the runs here are outstanding and more than an ample reward for the effort expended coming in.

The tour starts on Rt. 91 at a point 5¼ miles south of I-70. Park clear of the road right at the mouth of the gulch where highway 91 crosses Mayflower Creek. The initial part of the tour crosses private land but access has not been a problem and consideration should be shown concerning this.

Start skiing on the eastern side of the road, heading up the drainage. Ski east past some powerlines and along the right (south) side of the creek, climbing a steep hill. One soon comes to a sign designating a public access road. Go south along this passing some side roads near the 1 mile point of the tour. The road continues southeast into the main valley of Mayflower Gulch and stays to the right (southwest) of the creek all the way. For the next mile the trail climbs steadily but not too steeply and is in and out of the forest as it heads up the drainage. For almost another mile the trail then continues much the same along more open terrain with scattered trees. Then it heads out across a clear section to the old sight of the Boston Mine.

This is a cluster of buildings which are in quite good condition. Most parties will want to stop here briefly, even if they are going higher up the gulch. The bowls and hillsides beyond the cabins are obvious and as stated earlier, provide excellent powder runs. The return trip skis back down the same trail used on the ascent. If there is a lot of snow the last ¾ of a mile to the road can be skied directly down the streambed which is a bit nicer than descending the trail in this section.

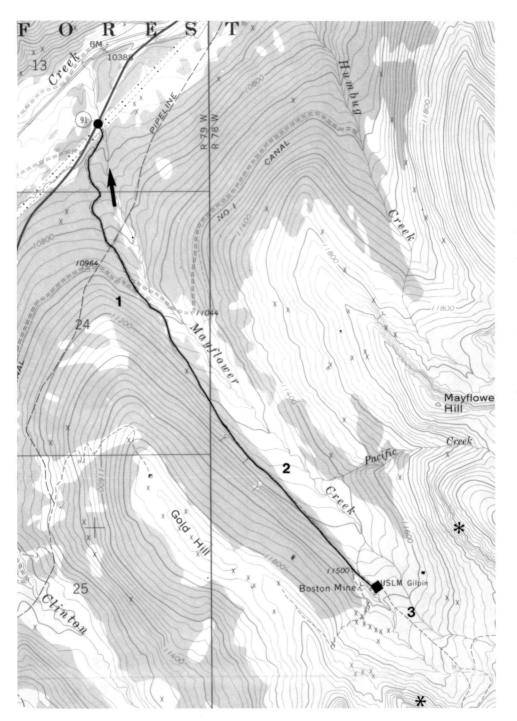

45 VAIL PASS-SHRINE PASS

Grade: Easy
Distance: 3 Miles—One Way
Elevation Change: 950 Feet
High Point: 11,530 Feet
Approximate Time: One-half Day
USGS Topographic Map:
  Vail Pass
  Redcliff

The rolling countryside and high open meadows of the Vail Pass area provide ideal terrain for cross-country skiing. Due to the high elevation and the large amounts of snow that fall here the season is often much longer than for many of the other tours described in this book. One can usually expect good skiing here from the middle of November until well into May. The Interstate passes right over Vail Pass and a large parking lot near the summit is plowed all winter which makes the access very straightforward. As the area does get a lot of snow, during stormy periods the road is often hazardous and during periods of bad weather it is wise to check road conditions before heading off to this area.

The tour described here is a short one that quite simply loops around out on the slopes to the northwest and west of the pass. It serves as a good introduction to the area and allows one to familiarize themselves with the terrain. One is virtually never out of sight of the pass or the Interstate so routefinding is not really much of a consideration. The descent back to the pass is moderate, fairly long, and a really fun run.

Reach the start of the tour by driving on I-70 to the summit of Vail Pass. Exit from the Interstate and park in the parking lot on the west side of I-70, just south of the exit.

Start skiing on the Shrine Pass road just west of the overpass across the Interstate. This is a good dirt road in the summertime and goes all the way to Redcliff. At first the road zigzags up the hillside to the northwest, but after two switchbacks it curves around to the southwest. Climb easily along the road which soon traverses the large south-facing hillside above West Ten Mile Creek. After one mile the road curves to the northwest and for one more mile it continues the long and steady climb. Then the road flattens out and one gets spectacular views across at the Gore Range which is off to the northeast. A short drop and climb brings one to the north side of a small dip beyond which the tour is flat for a ways as it heads northwest for ½ mile to Shrine Pass.

The pass really is just a long flat section of open clearings and not very distinct. The simplest and quickest way back to the car from here is to ski back down the road. A very pleasant and slightly longer alternative starts by heading west and then southwest from just before the pass and goes across to some woods below the main ridge. Then turn south and stay near the trees as one skis along keeping well below the steep slopes along the ridge. Ski south about one mile until one is due west of the parking area. Then start down the gradual and open slopes of the West Ten Mile Creek drainage. This long downhill run to the east takes the drainage, or the vague ridges bordering it, all the way back to the parking lot.

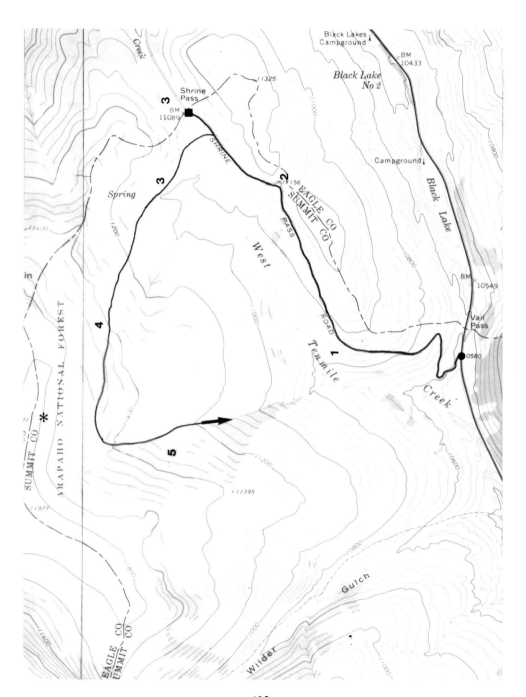

46 VAIL PASS TO REDCLIFF

Grade: Moderate
Distance: 11½ Miles—One Way Trip
Elevation Change: 1,670 Foot Loss
High Point: 11,160 Feet
Approximate Time: One Day
USGS Topographic Map:
  Vail Pass
  Redcliff

This tour follows a good summer dirt road. The skiing is nowhere difficult and after the initial 2½ miles of easy climbing the entire remainder of the tour is downhill. A large amount of the trip is out in the open with terrific views of the surrounding mountains, but the latter part of the trip is in a valley, fairly wooded, and sheltered. Despite the length, the tour normally goes quite quickly and the road is usually tracked by skiers or snowmobiles. Consequently this tour is excellent for developing skiers who are seeking a longer trip on easy terrain.

The tour terminates just outside of the town of Redcliff where a local Mexican restaurant serves as the "official" end of the outing for most skiers. Since Redcliff is rather out of the way and a long way from the starting point (about 30 miles by car) it is a good idea to spot a car here before starting or to make other plans for return transportation.

Reach the start of the tour by driving on I-70 to the summit of Vail Pass. Exit from the Interstate and park in a large lot on the west side of I-70 just south of the exit.

Start skiing on the Shrine Pass road just west of the overpass across the Interstate. This is a good dirt road in the summer time and it goes all the way to Redcliff. At first the road zigzags up the hillside to the northwest but after two switchbacks it curves to the southwest, climbing easily along the road which traverses the large south-facing hillside above West Ten Mile Creek. After one mile the road curves back to the northwest and for one more mile it continues the long and steady climb. Then the road flattens out and one gets spectacular views of the Gore Range which is off to the northeast. A short drop and climb brings one to the north side of a small dip beyond which the tour is flat for a ways as it heads northwest for ½ mile to Shrine Pass.

The pass really is just a long flat section of open clearings and is not very distinct. Then one starts down into the head of the Turkey Creek drainage. As one descends the valley curves to the west and after a total of 3¾ miles one reaches the overlook of the Mt. of the Holy Cross. This is marked by signs and an outhouse is located just off the road. Descend for another ¼ mile and pass a side road turning off to the right (Timber Creek Road). The next 3½ miles continues down along the right (north) side of the open meadows and wanders in and out of the woods along the north side of Turkey Creek. At the 7½ mile point one passes some old buildings and crosses to the south side of the stream. Beyond this is another 2 miles of steady descent through the forest and then the road recrosses Turkey Creek to its north side.

Soon one passes a turnoff to the south, near a bridge which heads off up Wearyman Creek. Three-quarters of a mile further one passes a gaging station and then the valley narrows down. One mile further on one passes a large water tank and comes to the point to which the road is plowed from the west. Continue along this for one more mile to reach the town of Redcliff.

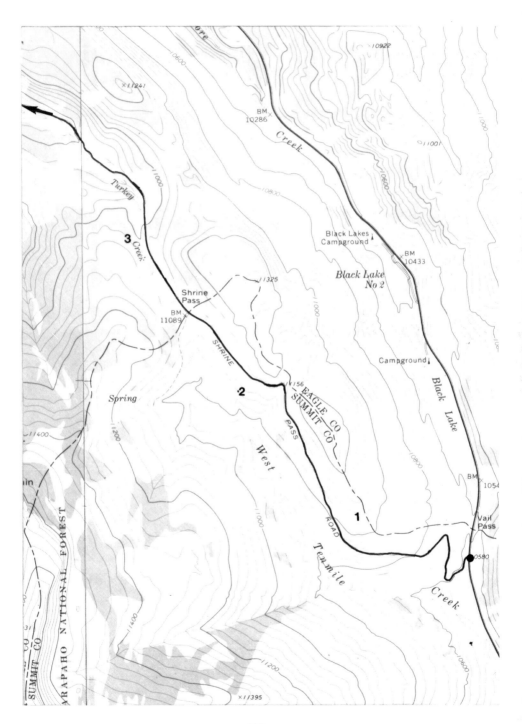

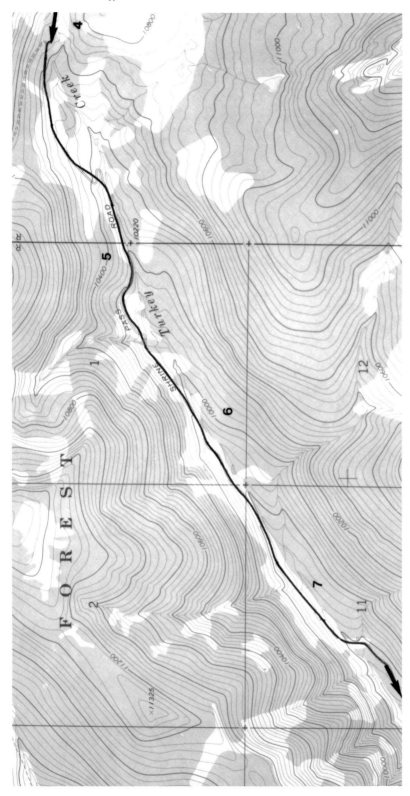

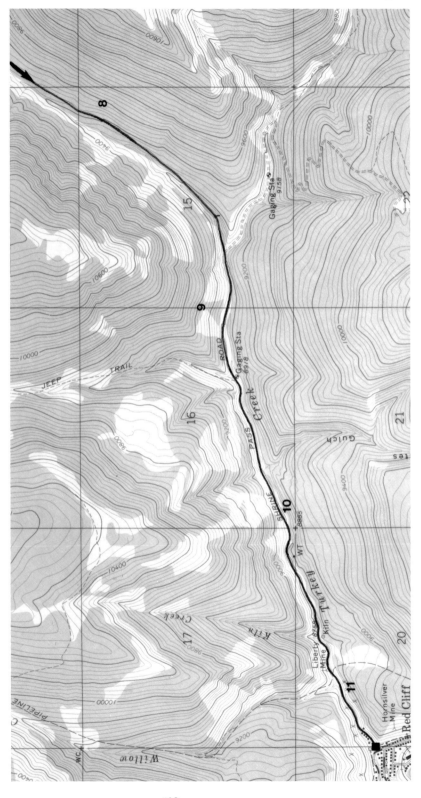

47 VAIL PASS TO VAIL

Grade: Difficult
Distance: 18 Miles—One Way Trip
**Elevation Change: 1,240 Foot Gain and a
2,340 Foot Loss**
High Point: 11,186 Feet
Approximate Time: One Full Day
USGS Topographic Map:
 Vail Pass
 Redcliff
 Vail East

The Vail Pass to Vail tour is universally held in highest regard and by many it is considered as the finest ski tour in Colorado. It is long and varied, it stays at a high elevation for almost its entire length, and in addition to the excellent skiing along the tour itself it ends at the Vail Ski Area, so the last section descends the ski runs there. As much of the skiing is along an open ridgeline the tour is very exposed to the elements. However this also results in absolutely magnificent views of all the surrounding mountain ranges and scenery.

It is also refered to as the 18 Mile Run and the Commando Run. The former appelation is due to the distance covered while the latter name as well as some of the names given to features along the trip stem from its usage in years gone by as a training run for the 10th Mt. Division. Not too long ago the Vail Pass to Vail trip was usually done as an overnight outing. In recent years the tour has become much more popular and is almost always tracked. This results in it being a much easier and faster trip and so most parties now find it quite reasonable to do in one long day.

With the increase in the number of skiers doing this trip there has been a tendency to downgrade its length and difficulty. One should be aware of the distances involved, the elevation at which the tour is situated, and the nature of the terrain covered. While the routefinding is not particularly difficult, inexperienced skiers or those not familiar with the tour sometimes have problems. These are usually encountered near the middle part of the route and are caused by a tendency to wander down off the ridgeline. The trip tends to naturally break into three sections. The first follows the Shrine Pass road, the next climbs up to the top of Pt. 11,710′ and continues along the ridgeline to Pt. 11,816′ or "Siberia Peak", and the third leads on to the Vail Ski Area and down that. The last third of the trip is virtually all downhill and goes rather quickly, ending at the base of the Vail Ski Area. If one arrives before the lifts close it is very reasonable to hitch a ride back to Vail Pass. In any event one must plan for return transportation from Vail to Vail Pass.

Reach the start of the tour by driving on I-70 to the summit of Vail Pass. Exit from the Interstate and park in the large lot on the west side of I-70 just south of the exit.

Start skiing on the Shrine Pass road just west of the overpass across the Interstate. This is a good dirt road in the summer and goes all the way to Redcliff. At first the road zigzags up the hillside to the northwest but after two switchbacks it curves to the southwest. Climb easily along the road which soon traverses the large south-facing hillside above West Ten Mile Creek. After one mile the road curves to the northwest and for one more mile it continues the long and steady climb. Then the road flattens out and one gets spectacular views of the

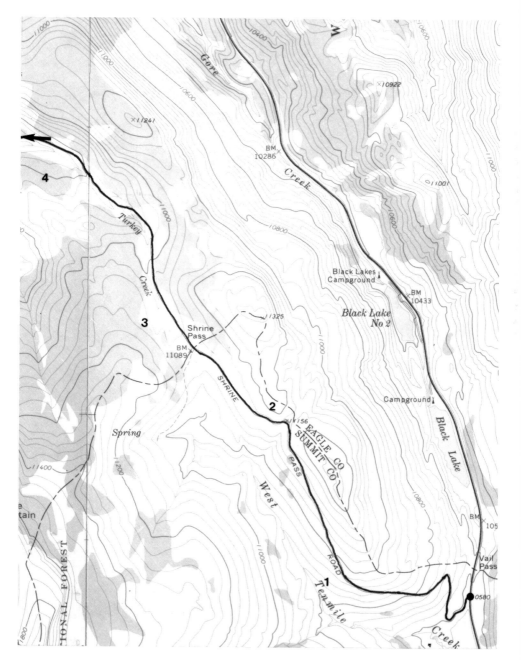

Gore Range which is off to the northwest. A short drop and climb brings one to the north side of a small dip beyond which the tour is flat for a ways as it heads northwest for ½ mile to Shrine Pass.

The pass really is just a long flat section of open clearings and is not very distinct. Then one starts down into the head of the Turkey Creek drainage. A long downhill run ensues which is quite fast when packed. As one descends the valley curves to the west and after a total of 3¾ miles one reaches the overlook of the Mt. of the Holy Cross. This is marked with signs and an outhouse is located just off the road. For the next ¼ mile the road descends more steeply and as it curves left at the bottom of the hill at a clearing a side road (Timber Creek Road) turns off to the right. Turn onto this and climb steadily up along it for ½ mile. Then the road forks and one should take the left-branch which is marked as Lime Creek Road. Very soon the woods give way to clearings and one reaches a large hillside up to the right with many scattered trees. This is the southeast flank of Pt. 11,611′ and is one of the two big climbing sections of the tour. Ascend the hillside, eventually aiming roughly for its upper left corner. There one reenters the woods and continues climbing steadily. The best route from this point is to keep contouring left (west) as one climbs and actually bypass the summit of Pt. 11,611. This course brings one onto the forested ridgeline west of Pt. 11,611′ at about the 6 mile point of the tour.

Ski west along the ridge for ½ mile and then up another short section of climbing. Here one comes to the high open clearings on Pt. 11,710′. These run to the northwest and the views from here are superb. Ski to the northwest end of the clearings along the crest of the ridge. At this point head to the northeast, staying with the ridgeline, and descend sharply to a heavily wooded saddle on the ridge. Continue to the northeast across this toward Pt. 11,618′. Many parties stray too far to the left in this section and are lured down into the drainage to the northwest. The best route stays pretty close to the crest of the ridge across the saddle and then climbs up the vague ridge leading up towards Pt. 11,618′. A few hundred feet below the top

of this point one can easily contour along the left (west) side of the ridge to bypass the actual highpoint and rejoin the ridgecrest just north of it. Then ski down the wooded ridge. As this heads north, this long descent ot Two Elk Pass can be one of the best runs of the trip.

From the broad and open glades of Two Elk Pass one can see the back bowls of Vail off to the northwest and the next section of the tour is all too obvious. Head north, climbing the open and seemingly endless south slopes of Pt. 11,816′. This is the highest point on the entire tour and is also often refered to as "Red Peak" and "Siberia Peak". As the eastern edge of this slope ends at a cliff band and is often badly corniced it is best to stay well away from that area. At the summit of this point one is at the eastern end of a long and very narrow ridge that runs west all the way to the top of the Vail Ski Area.

Those opting for this route to the area should ski along the crest of the narrow ridge until the way is blocked by a low band of cliffs. A pair of crossed sticks marks a tight cleft that allows easy descent through this band of rock and beyond this obstacle the rest of the route to the top of the ski area is straightforward. The last leg of this route descends to the north, down the downhill ski runs of the area to reach Vail, at the base of the mountain.

From Pt. 11,816′ most parties prefer not to follow the ridge to the west but use the following route instead. This starts be descending north along a broad ridge and following a line of clearings. This leads one above the east end of the Mill Creek drainage and after ½ mile one veers off to the left and begins the long and steep drop into this valley. This section, known as Mushroom Bowl, offers the best downhill runs of the entire trip. The further to the north one goes the easier the angle of descent becomes. Near the bottom of the bowl head north a bit toward the right side of the drainage and locate and old road. For the next 2½ miles one skis to the west along this road as it descends the Mill Creek drainage and leads to the Golden Peak lift of the Vail Ski Area.

Beyond the lift another ¾ miles of skiing continues down the road as it curves to the right and leads on to the downhill slopes. Descend these to reach the base of the mountain and Vail.

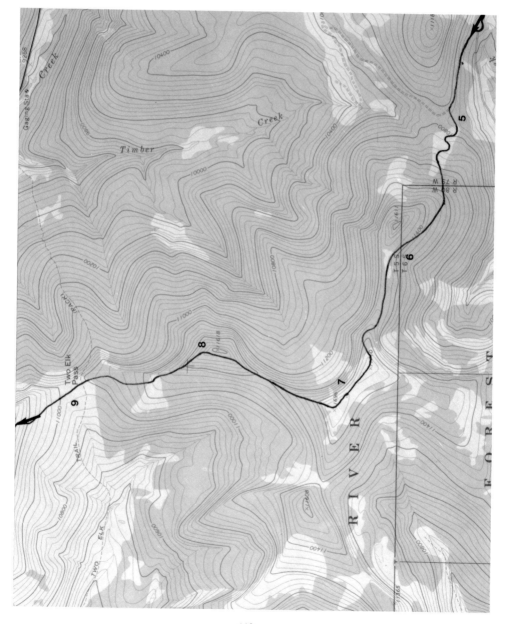

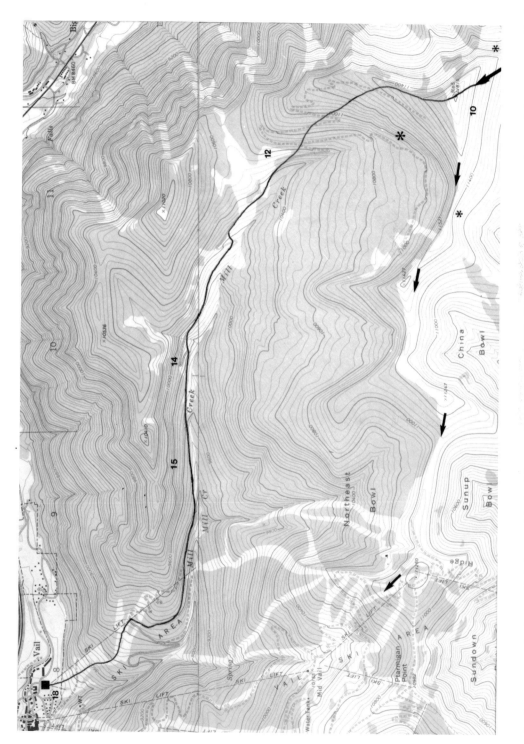

48 CONUNDRUM HOT SPRINGS

Grade: Difficult
Distance: 11 Miles—One Way
Elevation Change: 2,610 Feet
High Point: 11,200 Feet
Approximate Time: 1-2 Days
USGS Topographic Map:
  Aspen
  Hayden Peak
  Maroon Bells

The trip in to Conundrum Hot Springs is one of the most popular summer hikes in the state. In winter, while it is still a frequently visited spot the number of users drops off drastically. Though the tour has technically easy skiing the entire way, the very long distance covered (11 miles each way) mays it a rather strenuous and serious undertaking. The tour follows the valley bottom of Conundrum Creek and for most of the trip it stays on a jeep road. Although the valley itself is fairly flat it is quite deep and narrow in sections. Consequently portions of the trip are exposed to avalanches and caution is advised. While some parties will do this tour in one very long day most skiers will prefer to camp overnight. The latter group should note that no camping is permitted within one mile of the hot springs themselves.

Drive ½ mile north of Aspen on Rt. 82 and turn south onto a road marked for Maroon Lake and Ashcroft. Almost immediately the road forks and one should take the left-hand branch. Drive up this for 5 miles. Here, on the west side of the road is a sign marking the start of the trail up Conundrum Creek.

Start skiing down to the west along a road that soon crosses Castle Creek. The first ½ mile crosses private property as the road angles to the southwest and crosses to the left side of Conundrum Creek. Continue up the valley through the woods and after 1½ miles the main valley heads south. All the rest of the way the tour continues along this valley floor following the jeep road or the stream. The skiing is along a series of open meadows with sporadic sections of trees and the climb is very continuous but very gradual. At the six mile point one passes Cataract Creek which comes in from the east. Beyond this the valley narrows and for the next 1½ miles the gradient of the valley floor steepens a bit.

Then the valley opens out again and one passes a series of large clear hillsides up to the west. At the 8 mile point one goes by a summer pack trail that heads up the steep east side of the valley. ¼ mile further on one comes to Silver Dollar Pond. Continue south up the valley and after a total of 11 miles reach the Conundrum Guard Station cabin on the west side of the creek. Ski about a hundred yards further to a fork in the trail with a sign. Just up to the left are the hot springs, on the east side of Conundrum Creek. The return trip skis north, back out the valley to the road, and retraces ones tracks along the route.

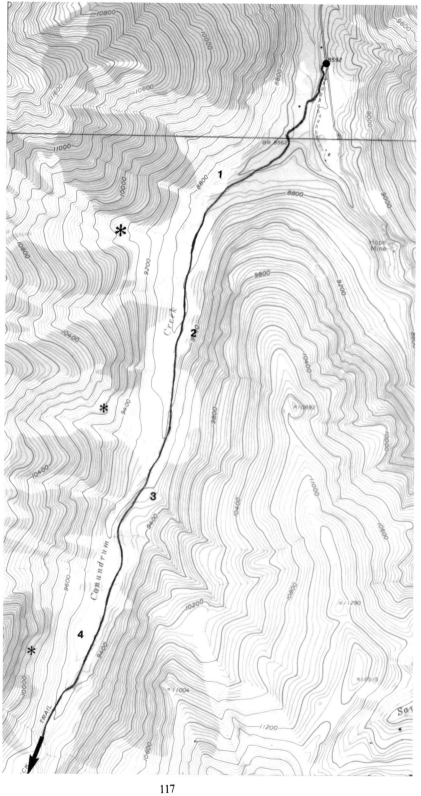

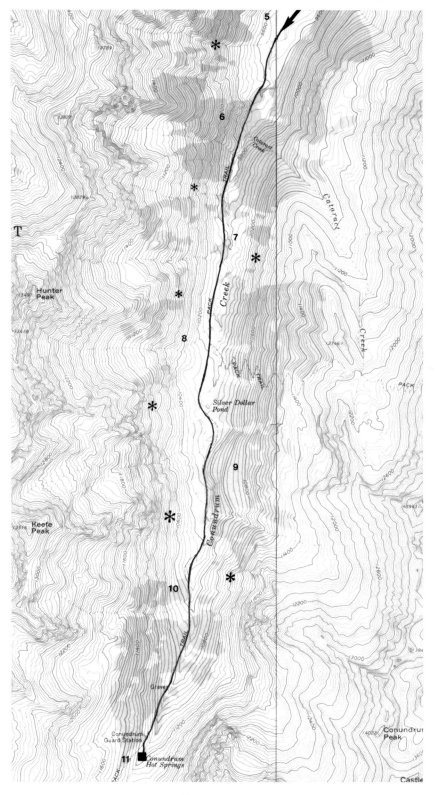

49 EXPRESS CREEK

Grade: Moderate
Distance: 4½ Miles—One Way
Elevation Change: 1,775 Feet
High Point: 11,200 Feet
Approximate Time: One Day
USGS Topographic Map:
  Hayden Peak

Undoubtedly much of the cross-country skiing in the Aspen area centers around the old townsite of Ashcroft. In addition to the touring center located there, it serves as the starting point for numerous backcountry tours. The attractions of the nearby valleys are enhanced by the presence of numerous huts of the Alfred Braun Hut System. The Markley Hut part way up Express Creek is one of these. This hut system is operated for the USSA by Alfred Braun. They are available to the public for a small fee and are on a reservation system. For full details as to the location of the various huts, the fees, reservations, and availability contact Alfred Braun, 702 W. Main St., Aspen Colorado 81611. The telephone number is (303) 925-7162.

The steady climb up to Express Creek is fairly sheltered and usually has good snow. Although it is described as stopping two miles beyond the Markley Hut more experienced skiers may wish to extend the tour by continuing beyond this point. As described here it is a good introductory tour to the Ashcroft area.

Drive ½ mile north of Aspen on Rt. 82 and turn south onto a road marked for Ashcroft and Maroon Lake. Almost immediately this divides and one should take the left branch and drive up this for 11 miles to Ashcroft. Here there is a touring center and a large parking on the east side of the road.

Start skiing from the parking area and go southeast across a meadow. Then cross Castle Creek and ski north a short way along the east side of the creek to intersect the jeep road that goes up Express Creek. This point is only ¼

mile from the parking area. Alternatively one can walk north along the main road for ¼ mile from the parking area to where the Express Creek jeep road turns off to the east. Ski southeast on this and cross Castle Creek to reach the same point mentioned above.

Whichever start is chosen, from the east side of the creek the road leads south as it goes uphill at a steady rate of climb. After another ½ of a mile the Waterfall Gulch stream, which comes down from the east, is crossed. This is the first of several small streams crossed in this section. Continue along the steep west-facing hillside past several open chutes and gulches as one climbs above the Castle Creek valley. After 1½ miles from the start of the trip the road curves to the left (southeast) and enters the Express Creek valley. ½ mile further there is a turnoff to the right (south) which leads down and across Express Creek to the Markley Hut. This A-frame cabin makes a good stopping point. If one wishes to ski further up Express Creek there is a choice of two routes, both of which are fairly close to each other. One is to not go to the hut but to keep skiing along the main jeep trail. This goes along the northeast side of the valley and soon crosses some big open slopes. After another couple of miles of steady climbing one reaches a steeper section beyond which the trail curves left (northeast) again. Taylor Pass lies just up to the southeast from here. This tour is described as ending here though it is reasonable to continue further up the valley as it levels out and eventually one can ski on to reach the Goodwin-Greene or Barnard Huts.

The other choice of routes is to go to the Markley Hut and then ski southeast up the streambed or along its south side for a couple of miles. Then cross the stream to rejoin the road at the point described above. The return trip skis back down ones tracks to reach the parking area at Ashcroft.

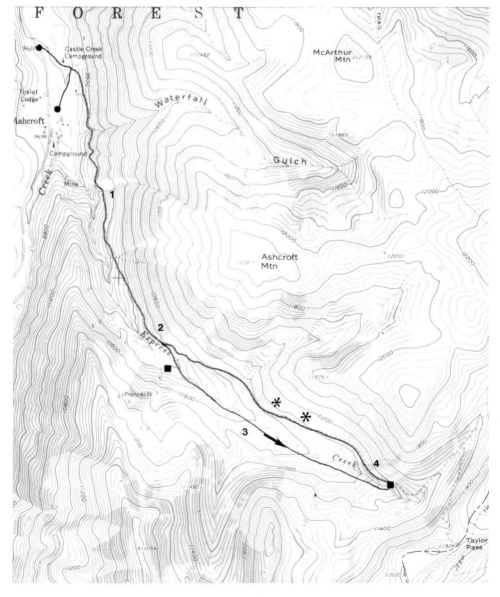

50 ASPEN TO CRESTED BUTTE VIA PEARL PASS

Grade: Difficult
Distance: 25 Miles—One Way Trip
Elevation Change: 3,207 Feet With a Net Loss
of 578 Feet
High Point: 12,705 Feet
Approximate Time: 2 Days
USGS Topographic Map:
  Hayden Peak
  Pearl Pass
  Gothic
  Crested Butte

The Aspen to Crested Butte trip is the longest and most demanding tour described in this book. While it is sometimes done as a very long one day trip, especially late in the season, it is most often done as an overnight outing. Many parties take advantage of the Tagert Hut and spend the night there. This does make the second day quite long but cuts down significantly on the amount of gear that must be carried. For information concerning the use of the hut contact Alfred Braun, 702 W. Main St., Aspen, Colorado 81611. Telephone number is (303) 925-7162. One should not underestimate the distance involved and especially if there is much new snow or the tour has not been tracked, then the possibility of spending a second night out is not out of the question. The steep-sided valleys of this trip pose a potential threat of avalanch hazard and care should be exercised when this situation exists.

The tour is described as going from Aspen to Crested Butte, the direction in which it is most commonly done, although it is not unusual to do the trip the other way. Since the tour terminates a long way from the start, the return trip must be planned for in advance. A car shuttle is not entirely satisfactory due to the inordinate amount of driving necessitated. When the route

over McClure Pass is drivable this reduces the road distance considerably. Another alternative is to retrace the tour and ski back to the starting point. This takes as long as the initial trip. In past years many skiers have had friends meet them at the end of the trip, driving around after letting them off at the start. Another popular alternative has been to take advantage of private flying services in either Aspen or Crested Butte and the luxury of flying back to the starting point is perhaps the most appealing choice. The availability and cost of such flights varies and one is advised to check with local air services beforehand.

The tour actually extends from Ashcroft to a point several miles outside of the town of Crested Butte. Leaving a car at Ashcroft is not a problem, though it is best to inform the people at the touring center. The short distance in to Crested Butte at the end of the trip can be walked or easily hitched. The fine mountain scenery, the good skiing, and the uniqueness of a long trip connecting two major ski resort towns all combine to make this a highly sought after and memorable outing.

Drive north of Aspen on Rt.82 for ½ mile and turn left onto a road marked for Ashcroft and Maroon Lake. Almost immediately the road divides and one should take the left fork and drive up this for 11 miles to Ashcroft. Park on the east side of the road in the large parking area of the Ashcroft Touring Center.

From the touring center buildings ski south on a jeep road that heads up the Castle Creek valley. Cross open fields on the touring center trails, passing buildings and fences. Then the road goes in and out of some clumps of trees to the west of the creek. After 1½ miles one passes the Pine Creek Campground and the road divides but soon reunites. This section is all

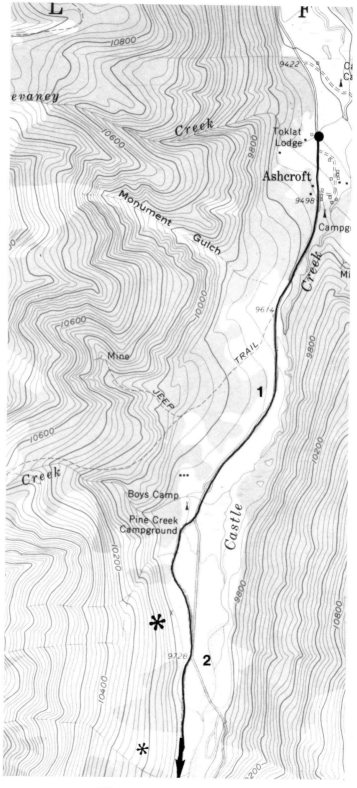

quite flat and at the 2 mile point the road forks. Take the right-hand road, though for the next mile both roads run parallel to each other up the valley. Then the valley divides and the left-hand road heads south up the Cooper Creek drainage. Take the narrower, right-hand valley and ski up this along Castle Creek. The road crosses to the south side of Castle Creek and starts climbing more steadily. The trail goes through clumps of trees as the valley narrows some more and ½ mile from the fork of the drainages one passes some cabins. These are near the road and are on the south side of Castle Creek. The remaining ½ mile to the Tagert Hut climbs much more steeply as the trail turns to the northwest and crosses the stream and then heads southwest as it zigzags up a steep hill. Near the top of this one turns left (east) to arrive at the hut. This small A-frame cabin is nestled in among trees on a small overlook. From the hut ski south, climbing uphill and rising above the treeline. Then head southeast ascending open and moderate slopes. After ½ mile the terrain levels off somewhat and one should contour along the gradual hillside on a southeasterly course. After another mile this brings one into a broad basin below Pearl Pass. It is best to stay well out to the east in this basin to avoid the steep walls and gullies along the western edge of the valley. A short steep climb then leads to Pearl Pass.

At Pearl Pass the summer jeep road heads southwest and crosses over a ridge into the upper end of another drainage. The best route does not follow this. Instead ski southeast down into a big open basin below the pass. If one swings out to the left (east) the angle of the slope is slightly less steep. From the pass, 1½ miles of fast and continuous downhill brings one to the treeline at the upper end of the East

Brush Creek valley, east of Carbonate Hill. Continue down into the valley along the streambed. For those not using the Tagert Hut this area offers good potential camping spots. Descend the valley for 1½ miles following the stream and then the drainage heads more to the southwest. After another 2 miles on this course, either along the creek or on the trail on its west side, the route curves sharply to the right. Descend a short steep section through the woods below which the jeep trail descends steadily to big clearings in the main Brush Creek valley. Go left (southwest) across these clearings and take the road along the right (northwest) side of the meadows until the valley narrows. Here one can either go directly down the steep and narrow defile of the creekbed for a short way or stay with the jeep road which goes along the steep slope up and above the north side of the creek. Either route soon leads on to the flatter sections of the valley below with its big open meadows and scattered glades of trees.

Continue skiing on past a large drainage coming in from the north and then head southwest across the open floor of the valley. Pass several old buildings and come to the junction of the Brush Creek and the East River valleys. The back side of the Crested Butte Ski Area is 1 mile to the northwest from here. Go south down the flat valley floor of the East River drainage and after 2 more miles one reaches the Cold Spring Ranch. The last couple miles are usually tracked by day tourers from Crested Butte. The Cold Spring Ranch consists of several large buildings and is at the end of a good road leading out to Rt. 135. This road is often plowed and it is 3 miles from the ranch to the main road. At the highway (Rt. 135) turn right (northwest) and proceed along this for just over 2 miles to the town of Crested Butte.

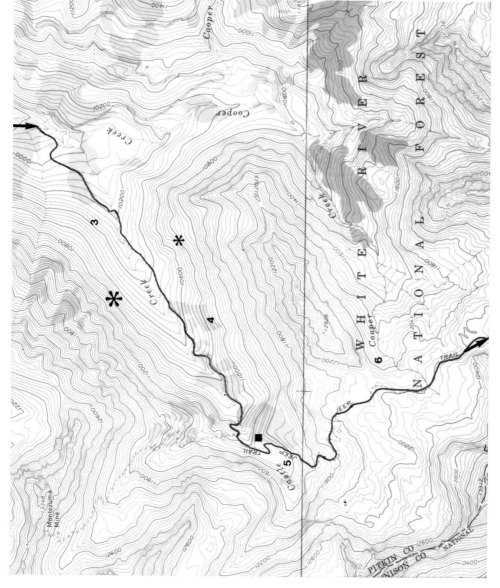

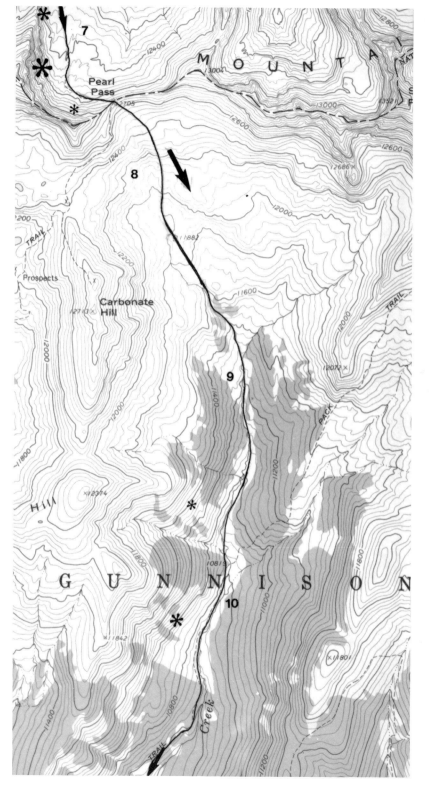

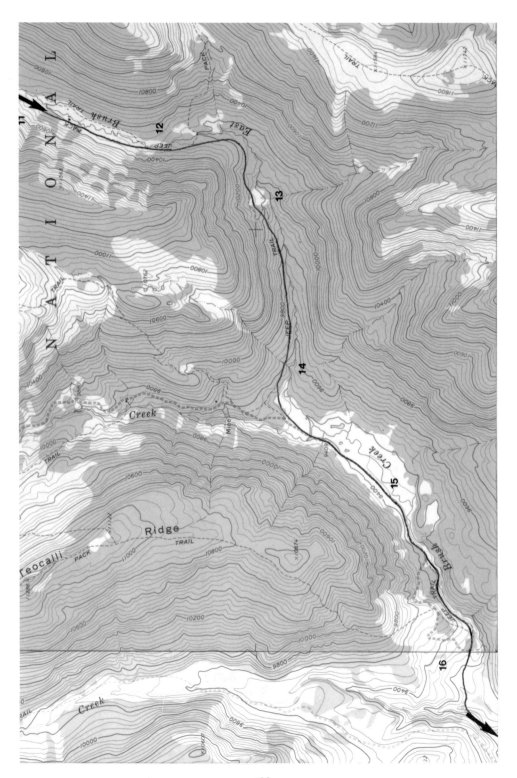

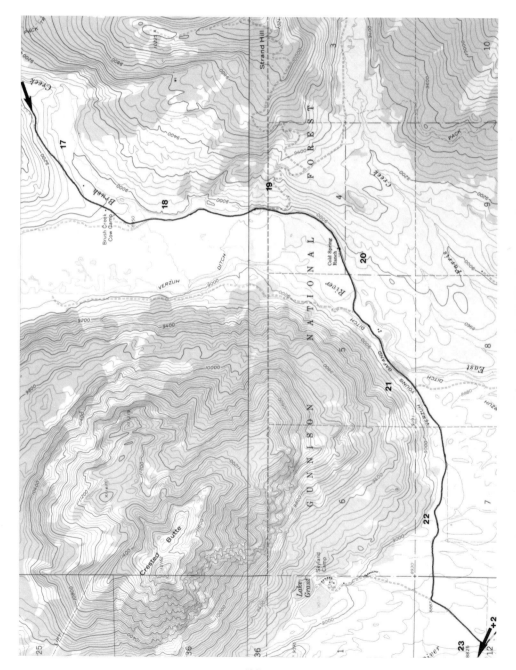